CW00447110

GREEN
LIVING

GREEN LIVING

Personal action to save our environment

David Green

**KOGAN
PAGE**

First published in 1990

Apart from any fair dealing for the purposes of research or private
study, or criticism or review, as permitted under the Copyright,
Designs and Patents Act, 1988, this publication may only be
reproduced, stored or transmitted, in any form or by any means, with
the prior permission in writing of the publishers, or in the case of
reprographic reproduction in accordance with the terms of licences
issued by the Copyright Licensing Agency. Enquiries concerning
reproduction outside those terms should be sent to the publishers at
the undermentioned address:

Kogan Page Limited
120 Pentonville Road
London N1 9JN

© David Green 1990

The right of David Green to be identified as author of this work has
been asserted by him in accordance with the Copyright, Designs
and Patents Act 1988.

British Library Cataloguing in Publication Data
A CIP record for this book is available from the British Library.

ISBN 0-7494-0266-0

Printed and bound in Great Britain by
Biddles Limited, Guildford

Contents

Preface

We take as our starting point the current state of the environment. It is not what we would wish it to be. World population is increasing, resources are diminishing, and pollution damage proliferates. The rate at which the environment is deteriorating due to these influences is so rapid that no government is likely to respond with measures sufficient to clean up the world's production act. Even if we have the resources to respond, we no longer have the time.

Despite this, too many people still believe that adopting less harmful production processes will solve our problems in due course. Some of the damage caused by production is being reduced and will be reduced even more, but this is not sufficient to halt the deterioration in our vital life-support systems. We are too far down the wrong road to neutralise production damage quickly enough.

We have one other option: to tighten the screws from the consumer end; to mobilise the power which each of us has to keep in check the demand that leads to damaging production processes. We have every incentive to do this; it is our skins that are on the line.

This book concentrates on this consumer approach. The first six chapters review the primary causes of environmental damage and consider some consumer options for containing it. The seventh looks at the state of play with regard to the greenhouse effect and ozone depletion, the consequences we can expect, and how we might shield ourselves from some of them. The eighth deals in detail with environmentally beneficial measures within our grasp in and about our own homes. Specific items included in previous chapters are restated.

This combination of a study of the key components of world environmental damage and a latter-day environmental version of Mrs Beeton's principles of household management is deliberate. A good understanding of the relationship between the two is essential if enough of us are to perceive, and react to, our pivotal role as ultimate consumers in all environmental damage.

In choosing the title for this book, I realised that the coincidence with my surname might suggest that one or other had been adopted merely for convenience. But the title sums it up more concisely and accurately than would any other; and the name was mine long before 'Green' became shorthand for anything else.

Many of the ideas which have inspired this text predate modern concerns by a long way. I first became sensitive to the realities of environmental damage in 1944 when my family moved from remote countryside to a northern city, which was filthy after a century of industrialisation made worse by the neglect and dereliction of war. The shock of that contrast haunted me ever after.

The substance of this book owes much to the ever extending enquiry which that shock engendered, and to later working experience in many fields relevant to the environment. It owes a great deal to talented specialists – friends and colleagues – who, over the years, patiently fielded technical questions. Foremost among those – and this may surprise dedicated Greens – were the highly talented members of the multi-disciplinary team with which I was fortunate to work during my 10 years in the British nuclear power industry. I am grateful to all of them.

I would like to acknowledge assistance on detail from the works of the authors listed on pages 140–41; to thank ICI's technical products manager at Mond House, Northwich for telling me a lot about the soda industry; and in particular to thank my daughter Pom. She bore philosophically my almost total withdrawal from our domestic life while I was researching and writing this text; she also helped significantly with a computation which needed more maths, physics and chemistry than I possess, as well as the ability to operate a calculator which would handle runs of figures with more than 25 zeroes on the end.

David Green

July 1990,
Castle Morris,
Pembrokeshire,
SA62 5EJ

1

Hard Realities

'During the next hour . . . 500,000 tonnes of coal will come out of the bituminous and lignite mines of the world . . . over two million barrels of crude oil, or about 300,000 tonnes will be extracted, with one giant tanker leaving a port every hour . . . nearly 200 million cubic metres of natural gas will be gathered . . . and one billion kWh of electricity will be transmitted from power plants – energy which could light up 10 billion 100-watt electric bulbs.'

Vaclav Smil: *Energy–Food–Environment* (1987)

It is only we – the ultimate consumers – who can solve the problems of resource depletion; and of the pollution created by the use of those resources which increasingly threatens our health and our lives. Only we as individuals can take the myriad of small precautions, and achieve the myriad of small economies in our own lives which will add up to the vast reduction in resource usage, waste and pollution upon which our own survival depends.

Governments will not do it – certainly not on their own. They can only act on the large scale, imposing general restrictions which might cause unnecessary hardship and resentment because they do not distinguish between the infinite variety of individual circumstances. In any case, the main concern of governments is to survive for the term of their natural life – five years or so – which is a lot shorter than the natural life most of us would hope for. They are not likely to impose restrictions or incur expenditure which will bite hard during their lifetime in order to spare a different government from having to take more desperate measures in 10, 15 or 20 years' time.

9

Governments may be sensitive to our general views – every five years or so when they seek our votes. But between times they compromise on a daily basis with powerful, sectional vested interests which may have little to do with any general view. We, on the other hand, can pursue a consistent course; and if we choose to take care of the environmental cents and pennies, the dollars and pounds will take care of themselves. No one can afford to ignore the effect of resolute consumer resistance – as the British government discovered recently with the cattle disease BSE.

One needs only to look at a few recent events to appreciate the limitations of government action. In 1975 the European Commission gave European Community members 10 years to eliminate pollution and associated health risks on bathing beaches. Fifteen years later, Britain is being prosecuted for doing nothing. So are most of the other countries concerned. In 1990, the world's leading meteorologists concluded unanimously that the build-up of greenhouse gases from the world's power stations and motor vehicles threatened a runaway heating of the earth's atmosphere. They reported that only an immediate 60 per cent reduction of gases would stabilise even the 1990 position. America reacted by challenging the experts' conclusions, and by saying that in any event, compliance was impossible since it would cost more than the total US national product. Britain merely offered to cut British emissions back to 1990 levels by 2005.

Even the widely trumpeted international agreement to protect the earth's ozone layer hides a sorry reality. Before the damaging CFCs are phased out under that agreement in the year 2000, there will have been a 30 per cent increase in their production worldwide.

For these reasons this study concentrates on measures we can adopt, in and from our homes, to cut back on the overall level of demand. For it is demand, to which each of us contributes, which drives the machine that is eating into our future more and more rapidly; and it is *our* future which is now at risk, not merely that of our children, or our children's children. Pollution is already striking at us locally, with vermin and disease breeding in waste dumps and foul watercourses, and toxic gases from vehicles and other sources present in the air we breathe; it is striking regionally through lakes, rivers and forests devastated by acid rain and water supplies corrupted by fertiliser run-off and algal growth; it is striking worldwide with the consequences of ozone depletion in the upper atmosphere and heating of the lower atmosphere – conditions examined in detail in Chapter 7.

As individuals, we can do something about all these perils. No one would open mines, drill for oil, smelt metals, erect and operate power stations, build factories or smother land with fertilisers, pesticides or weedkillers if we did not buy their products. The problems which result from the making and consumption of products would be eased overnight if we simply reduced the quantities we use.

Protesting alone is not enough. What, for example, was the achievement of the half a million Earth Day pilgrims who massed to demonstrate in New York in April 1990 but left 150 tons of litter behind them when they departed?

Before embarking on a course of Green Living, some basic factors should be borne in mind to help us to make informed judgements. They may seem obvious to some, but many people continue to act as though these concerns had nothing to do with them.

The production process

As consumers, we are remote from the original source of the materials which go into the articles we buy, and from the energy and materials which are consumed along the line between the source and ourselves. It therefore often requires a leap of the imagination to envisage the environmental impact and detailed background of the handy little article on the retailer's shelf. Yet everything on that shelf has such an impact and appreciating it is essential to the adoption of new disciplines on consumption.

A bird's eye view of two long-established manufacturing processes serves to illustrate the realities of all manufacture. The products which emerge into ordinary domestic life from these processes are bicarbonate of soda, washing soda, salt and bleach. They and other products start with common salt – sodium chloride – which is mined from the ground by pumping water down into rock salt and pumping back the resulting brine. Pumping conditions are carefully controlled to prevent land subsidence.

Bleach (sodium hypochlorite) is one of the products of a process which concentrates on the chlorine content of salt; washing soda and bicarbonate of soda are derived from a process which concentrates on the sodium content. So it is convenient shorthand to call them respectively the Chlorine and the Soda process.

Very large quantities of electricity are the key to the Chlorine process. Within sealed cells brine is pumped over electrically charged liquid mercury. Electrolysis releases two important industrial gases – hydrogen and chlorine – which must be scrupulously contained since the first is explosive and the second poisonous. Bleach is made (in a form far more concentrated than that in which we buy and use it domestically) when chlorine is stirred back into the brine solution.

The amounts of electricity required for the Chlorine process are so great that Chlorine process plants frequently have their own power stations. Waste power station heat (see Chapter 2, page 29) may then also be used to evaporate common salt for domestic consumption out of the basic brine feed stock.

A Chlorine process plant is likely to produce chlorine required for industrial processes and, when dissolved in small quantities, to kill bacteria in swimming pools and water supplies; industrial hydrogen; hydrochloric acid (made by burning hydrogen and chlorine together in water); and common salt and bleach used industrially and domestically. It is likely to be so designed and balanced that its only waste will be water, left after the brine feedstock has shed all its salt; and the combustion products from whatever fuel is burned in its power station. Its power station will be designed and run for the most efficient operation of the plant and that will include facilities for exchanging electricity with the national grid when the plant has a surplus or shortage. So such a plant will incorporate everything which human ingenuity can devise to make the most of resources, with the least damage to the environment. But the burning of energy – and its damage to the environment – is inescapable.

Large quantities of heat rather than electricity are the key to the

Soda process but a Soda process plant is also likely to include a power station whose heat can be used and whose electrical energy peaks and troughs can be exchanged with the national grid.

In the Soda process ammonia and carbon dioxide are forced into brine under pressure. They react and bicarbonate of soda forms leaving ammonium chloride once the bicarbonate is filtered out.

Ammonium chloride is used in the pharmaceutical industry and is the white substance found in ordinary torch batteries. Bicarbonate of soda is used in medicines as well as for cooking.

With more heat bicarbonate of soda converts into soda ash (sodium carbonate) which is used in glass making and washing powders. Dissolved in water soda ash crystalises as washing soda ready for domestic use when crushed and graded. In another form, soda ash is the basis of bath salts.

Heat is also needed to produce the ammonia and carbon dioxide with which the Soda process starts but the ammonia can be continuously recycled. The carbon dioxide is produced by burning quarried limestone, and some of the vast quarries surrounding Buxton in Derbyshire are mute memorials to the quantities required. Once the limestone has been burned quicklime remains; when that is heated with the ammonium chloride remaining in the original salt solution, the ammonia with which the process started is recovered.

The ultimate residue is calcium chloride. That has uses as diverse as an ingredient in pet foods, and in muds and fluids used in oil drilling.

Apart from the inescapable venting of energy combustion products, factories using either the Chlorine or Soda processes are likely to be as friendly to the environment as any industrial plant can be. In Western industrial countries they are usually subject to stringent environmental controls, long policed in the United Kingdom through the Alkali Inspectorate; but economics impose their own disciplines on any such plant in a competitive market. The cost of complicated processes itself inhibits waste.

The processes discussed in detail in the case of these two industries serve to emphasise why our demand for and use of the products of all industries matters so much. Every product requires energy, and burning that energy results in environmental

13

damage even if there is no other damage. If we buy less there is less damage.

Even our food represents energy burned. While it grows, a crop of corn will absorb energy from the sun so that it may, when ripe, contain four or more times the energy used to plant and cultivate it, and to make the fertilisers, weedkillers and pesticides that enhance yields. But by the time that corn has been harvested, transported, milled, processed, baked and delivered to us as bread, each calorie of energy in the bread has cost a calorie of man-made energy. Again, it takes energy to fertilise and periodically replant the grass which our cows eat; energy to grow and manufacture their supplementary feeds. The sun contributes to everything which grows, but once the cows have been milked, and their milk has been chilled, transported, pasteurised, bottled and delivered to us, each pint has nevertheless cost something like a pint of oil.

The impact of different living standards

We in Western industrialised countries have the most to answer for when it comes to the environment because we consume and pollute the most. The poorest people in the third world, living in countries where the gross annual national product may average no more than around $250 a head, cannot do much more harm to the environment than their own muscle allows. They must build their houses and shelters with their own labour and using materials found locally, which seldom involves any wider harm. They must find and carry their fuel from natural and renewable sources; fetch and carry their own water; crop and cultivate their own food; and return their wastes and that of their animals to the soil from which their food is grown. At worst, they can only abuse their immediate environment, and only that if their number, or the number of their livestock, increases beyond levels which that environment will sustain. If that happens, the abuse is brutally self-correcting: they starve.

We are at the other end of the scale. Our average national product may be between 50 and 100 times that of the world's poorest. Each one of us is responsible for at least 50 times the resource depletion and pollution of third world inhabitants. We take, and with our wealth are able to buy, everything we can lay our hands on. We throw back into the environment any part of it which we cannot use easily or dispose of cheaply. Because of the rate at which we draw on resources, the environmental impact of the 56 million people in the United Kingdom equals that of at least 2800 millions living at world subsistence level.

World population now exceeds 5000 million: but if you multiply the number in each nation by the extent to which its living standard exceeds that of the poorest countries, the impact of those 5000 million on world resources and environment is the equivalent of 53,000 million living at subsistence level.

Of course, the earth lacks both the space and subsistence level resources to support anything like 53,000 million people. It only sustains their equivalent, in the very different living standards of the existing 5000 million, because our skills have allowed us to harness to our advantage resources inaccessible to the poorest. By using those resources we are able to crowd ever larger numbers of people together in ever smaller spaces without risking their decimation by disease; and to multiply and use the earth's natural yields to feed, clothe and water them. But most of those resources are finite and we are exhausting them at a terrifying rate. Energy is the key to all of them; and though it took 400 million years of organic life to accumulate the earth's fossil fuels, we look set to burn them in less than 400 years.

The extent to which we have crawled out on to an increasingly fragile and environmentally dangerous energy limb, is illustrated by a simple comparison. In 1800 farmers in England considered that they were doing quite well, using subsistence methods, to grow and harvest between 3 and 5 hundredweights of barley or wheat on an acre of land (376 kg to 627 kg per hectare). With modern farm machinery, fertilisers, pesticides and weedkillers, farmers worldwide would now expect to cultivate between 3 and 6 tons to the acre (7526 kg to 15,052 kg per hectare). Without these advances, starvation would long since have kept in check national population increase along with world population increase; but starvation will still be there for many millions if energy usage has to be savagely reduced in order to preserve an atmosphere which will not destroy us, or if energy sources are exhausted.

Waste

The most obvious and least painful route to retaining a life such as we now enjoy, whose by-products would not threaten our survival, would be one which eliminated waste. It is hardly surprising that waste figures prominently in all studies concerned with saving the environment, and this one is no exception. But avoiding waste is a much wider issue than merely recycling; and avoiding pollution by waste involves a great deal more than setting up expensive measures to contain it.

Many people forget that by the time they come across something which can be defined as waste, most of the damage has been done and cannot be undone. Forests cut down to make paper, and the resources used to process it, are not redeemed by pouring in still more resources to reprocess it; nor is the waste apparent in used bottles recovered by burning more resources to put them in bottle-banks and reprocess them. As far as the environment is concerned, we must concentrate far more systematically on reducing the quantities used in the first place.

Another aspect of tunnel vision regarding waste is the failure to appreciate that our own time, energy and muscle power are resources which we waste ever more profligately in unproductive endeavours: we are like machines running on full power all the time but unfruitful for long periods. All of us could use more of our time producing goods and services for ourselves in our own homes, and achieve a corresponding reduction in the amount we contribute to the general market demand for those goods and services.

Perhaps most misguided of all is the view that the problems of waste and pollution can be solved merely by using still more resources to separate and contain them. This is no more than an extension of the 'not-in-my-back-yard' philosophy which has bedevilled past attempts at environmental improvement.

We did not like raw sewage flowing down our streets, so we piped it into sewers and channelled it into rivers or the sea. When the consequences of that appeared intolerable, we piped it further out to sea. We did not like the filthy black atmosphere over our cities, so we banned fuels and furnaces which produced obvious

16

black smoke and replaced them by ones which did not. We ignored the fact that we were still releasing the most damaging ingredients of black smoke – the invisible carbon, nitrogen and sulphur oxides and the acids which they form in combination with water. We made it easier to ignore them by building taller chimneys and sending the fumes further afield.

The rubbish we throw out and the places where we throw it do matter; but the sheer volume of waste which we are now creating makes any reasonable prospect of containment impossible. Britain alone produces 50,000 tonnes of solid domestic waste every day and for most of it there is no option but dumping in landfill sites. As the next chapter makes all too clear, even that volume will be dwarfed by the quantities of far more toxic waste which will have to be handled if resources are mustered to eradicate all harmful substances from power station chimneys.

The environment on which we depend does not have separate waste-disposal compartments. No matter how we manage our affairs, all waste has to be dumped somewhere, and wherever we choose to dump it there is a risk of harm. Reducing the volume of waste we create, and the quantity of commodities we consume whose manufacture results in waste, must therefore have an even higher priority than so-called waste treatment. As individuals we can and must reduce our contribution to the creation of waste.

Establishing priorities

We can assess the nature and extent of the environmental damage we cause from the nature, quality and quantity of the waste we throw out, the quantity of energy products we burn, and the way we burn them. If as consumers we buy goods for use in our homes or gardens which contain toxic substances, the packaging will carry instructions for their use and for the safe disposal of residues. However, it is far more difficult to judge the environmental damage caused by the manufacture of the articles we consider buying, and the extent to which we contribute to that damage by buying them. We will, for example, protect against environmental harm by using aerosols which are free of gases that damage the ozone layer; but how much harm has been caused already by the energy and resources used to make the aerosols?

17

The only simple and general yardstick is price. Price is admittedly a very crude guide. For example, it would only reflect the true environmental cost of raw materials from natural, non-renewable sources if manufacturers had to buy at replacement cost. Only materials which were wholly recycled and wholly attributable to renewable resources would come in that category, and no manufacturer is limited to those.

For all that, the cost of the goods we buy does reflect the efficiency with which manufacturers use resources, and has to cover everything actually spent on production, including the cost of complying with such general environmentally protective regulations as do exist. So the price of goods is a better measure of environmental cost and the damage inherent in production processes than anything else. The basic, general and simple rule of thumb therefore is that the more a particular category of products costs, the greater the environmental damage which producing it is likely to have caused.

Underpinning personal living standards

In 1990 the United Nations reported a further acceleration in the increase in world population which now tops an extra 100 million people every year. The extra demand that this will create, combined with diminishing resources, will lead to a steady increase in basic living costs during our lifetime. Worldwide measures to limit pollution damage will add to those costs.

These increases will progressively eat into real prosperity and living standards, in much the same way as the first worldwide surge in the price of oil and other commodities in the 1970s did, and that following the Iraqi invasion of Kuwait is likely to do now. So anyone who reconstructs his or her way of life so that it takes less out of and depends less on the general environment will also have a far better chance of sustaining that way of life. Environmental dangers are not the only ones which hang over our future.

An environmental diet

The most extreme advice which anyone concerned with saving the environment could give him or herself is much the same as that sometimes offered to people anxious about being over-weight: 'Stop consuming'. That is not practical or realistic – in either case. But the ordinary disciplines of dieting are. We can aim for a more balanced compromise between the 'take-all' way we do things now and the 'take-nothing' extreme; for a style of life which is not so significantly different as to be unacceptable, but which would nevertheless be far less damaging.

At its simplest, any dieting exercise can be reduced to a long catalogue of domestic dos and don'ts – some of which may seem very petty unless measured against the results which can be expected if large numbers of people adopt them. Such lists are published from time to time.

But above and beyond specific dos and don'ts, individual action to save the environment requires that individuals begin to think creatively about their own often unique and diverse ways of living. A prerequisite of this is an understanding of the basic mechanics of the way things are done; and of the way things that are harmful are already happening, and the knowledge that they may become more harmful. It is for that reason that this book combines both approaches. We may all benefit from specific suggestions; but to make any real contribution, we must understand the underlying logic.

Conclusions

Many writers have addressed environmental dangers on the global scale and are able to cite horrifying statistics. But unless we are willing to stand back and let it all wash over us, we must be able to relate the menace of those statistics to avoiding action which we can take as individuals. The main purpose of this book is to help to bridge that gap between the theoretical and the practical.

Whatever happens, the world environment will be the ultimate leveller: an environmental holocaust will not distinguish between rich or poor. The production of food and other manufactured and processed goods which we demand will inevitably draw still more on natural resources, burn still more energy, and create still more pollution. But while the earth can absorb and recover naturally from certain levels of pollution, the *total* of what we already create far exceeds those levels (as seen in the example of an immediate 60 per cent reduction needed in the output of greenhouse gases to stabilise atmospheric overheating at 1990 levels).

By voluntarily limiting the quantity of resources used and the burning of energy we can, as individuals, try to close the gap between what the environment can safely tolerate and what it cannot. It is up to us to do this, for no government or international action is likely to suffice.

2

The Energy We Use

We can reduce the amount of energy required to manufacture products simply by using fewer of them, avoiding their waste and using substitutes which require less energy .

We can significantly reduce the amount of energy which we burn directly. In part, that involves burning less – be it electricity, gas, oil, petrol, coal or any other solid fuel; in part, it involves using the most efficient form of energy and, where possible, that which has the least damaging side-effects on the environment.

Very few of us have sufficient information at our fingertips to make choices about the sort of energy we burn, and the form in which energy finally reaches us may not offer any reliable guide. For example, by the time electricity arrives in our homes it seems to be the cleanest of all forms of energy, and the fact that its price is fairly competitive suggests that its cost in terms of resources does not differ much from that of other fuels. Neither of these assumptions is true.

This chapter is concerned with the background to energy production and with some of the lesser-known facts.

Harnessing energy

Fuel could be burned very efficiently if we only used heat and only burned fuel to produce it where the heat is needed. It is possible to design domestic and industrial fuel-burning appliances in which as much as 85 per cent of the heat yielded by the fuel can be delivered for space or water heating, or for an industrial process. Only the remainder is vented as waste – along with any potentially harmful combustion products, of course.

The energy in fuel mostly has to be converted into mechanical energy before we can use it and inescapable physical laws make that conversion process inherently wasteful. Machines may be driven by gases, vapours or liquids. The vast proportion of the energy we use comes from burning or exploding fuel to produce gases or vapours to rotate steam or jet turbines, or move pistons in steam or oil engines.

Whatever the primary energy source, no machine will harness it unless the pressure on (or in) the gas or liquid which drives it is significantly higher when it enters the machine than when it leaves. So if you reverse your car into an earth bank and block the exhaust-pipe, you may find it impossible to start the engine. Pressure builds up in the exhaust as soon as the engine first fires: the difference between the pressure in the cylinders and the blocked exhaust is not then sufficient to turn the engine.

The amount of energy which a turbine or piston harnesses is measured by the difference between the high pressure of the flow of gas or liquid which enters it and the low pressure which leaves it. But because gas, vapour or water has to flow through to make machines run, it inevitably carries with it, unused, a substantial part of its original energy. A major part of the energy carried through is energy present in the form of heat rather than pressure.

If a substance has to be heated to create high pressure – water to steam, for example – energy is first lost merely in the heating process. More is then swallowed by friction in the machine which it drives; and a great deal is then lost with the waste products which escape at the low-pressure end. When petrol or oil are exploded in internal combustion engines, the heat created by the explosion is also lost. If machines vent directly into the low pressures of the general environment, as vehicle and aircraft engines do, these losses are irretrievable; but they are seldom recoverable even if the driving flow of gas or vapour is contained in a closed circuit, as with steam in a power station.

There must still be an adequate low-pressure zone beyond the turbine outlet in a closed-circuit power station system. This is created by running turbine exhaust steam through water-cooled condensers. These reconvert the steam into water which is then returned to the boilers for reheating. That process transfers the waste heat into vast quantities of cooling water, but for reasons discussed in the next section it is rarely recoverable.

22

Whether the device be turbine, windmill, piston or water-wheel, substantial wastage is unavoidable when harnessing energy. This is particularly true of the generation of electricity and we should exercise great care in the way we use it.

Electricity

The overwhelming proportion of the electricity made worldwide is generated from steam-driven turbines. The steam is produced in boilers heated by burning fossil fuel – coal, oil, or gas – or nuclear fuel. For reasons which will emerge later in this chapter, natural energy sources such as wind, water and solar power are unlikely ever to contribute more than a tiny fraction of the total quantity of energy needed. It is an illusion to believe that natural energies can solve our problems; and postponing the day when we face up to the implications of burning fossil or nuclear fuels is a luxury we cannot afford.

Megawatts always feature in any discussion of electricity, so it is helpful to define what they are and what they mean. A domestic iron or two-bar electric fire is generally rated at 1000 watts (one kilowatt – kW). The watt is the measure of the quantity of electricity required to power the appliance, so the higher the number of watts the more it consumes. If an appliance rated at 1000 watts is switched on for an hour it will burn one kilowatt hour (kWh) of energy. One kWh is the unit of electricity by which our electricity bills are calculated.

A megawatt (MW) is shorthand for a million kWh; so a power station which generates 1MW will produce enough electricity to keep 1000 1kW electric irons going for an hour. When the performance of different types of power station is compared, that of 1000MW stations is generally used as a standard.

The total generating capacity of all the power stations in England and Wales (ie ignoring Scotland and Northern Ireland) is approximately 60,000MW. More than 120 different stations contribute to that total, and many are smaller than the 1000MW standard.

Approximately two-thirds of that generating capacity is coal fired, capable of contributing around 40,000MW of the 60,000MW total. A few of the coal-fired stations have been

23

adapted to burn oil or gas as an alternative. Nuclear power station capacity accounts for 10,000MW of the remainder (about 18 per cent) oil-fired stations a little less. The rest comes from diesel, gas turbine, hydro-electric or hydro-electric pumped storage systems.

In pumped storage schemes electricity not require in low demand, off-peak periods is used to pump water up into a high-level reservoir. When reversed, the pumps function as water-powered turbine generators. Thus in periods of peak electricity demand, instant extra power is available by releasing the reservoir water back down through the pump-generators.

This to-ing and fro-ing with water makes it possible to store unwanted electricity from fossil and nuclear power stations, which cannot be turned on and off at the drop of a hat, and to convert it into hydro-electric power, which can.

If a country has no sufficient natural source of instant hydro-electric energy to meet peak electricity demand, as is Britain's case, pumped storage may be preferable to burning gas or oil in diesel or jet engine-powered generators, which also respond very quickly. It is certainly preferable to covering peak demand with more fossil fuel or nuclear capacity not needed at all in off-peak periods. But pumped storage schemes nevertheless add yet more to the energy, resource and environmental cost of the electricity they ultimately produce. They are no answer to our problem.

Some countries generate a far higher proportion of their electricity with nuclear power. France leads the field with around 65 per cent nuclear generation; Belgium (60 per cent) and Sweden (50 per cent) come second and third. Countries such as Norway, which have the right natural conditions, generate a large proportion of their electricity from hydro-electric schemes. But with a population of around three million, Norway's total energy needs are low. As far as the rest of the world is concerned, British dependence on fossil fuels is fairly typical.

Power stations fuelled by coal, oil, nuclear or other heat energies are inflexible because they must first raise steam before they can generate, and because frequent wide temperature fluctuations spell a very short life for furnaces and boilers. They cannot be started up at a moment's notice, nor can they be regularly started and stopped economically. They are shut down

24

periodically, in carefully controlled conditions, for maintenance and repair, but are essentially designed to keep running all the time. Generally speaking, sufficient are kept running to provide enough electricity to meet the average need – the base load.

Stations which can be brought to full power very quickly – diesel, gas turbine, hydro-electric or pumped storage – meet peak demands. In many countries, however, (and certainly in Britain) base-load capacity still significantly exceeds that required round the clock. So although great skill and ingenuity is used to balance electricity generation and limit waste, fuel burned in base-load stations may still be entirely wasted as generating continues through periods of very low demand.

It is because of this that efforts are made to encourage the use of electricity outside peak periods by offering cheap rates. Britain's off-peak White Meter electricity is an example. But that electricity still costs the same in resources and pollution. Marketing off-peak electricity for space and water heating does not eliminate the waste inherent in using electricity instead of more appropriate fuels for these purposes. If it did, there would be no need to cut the price in order to make it competitive.

It might seem a better answer to link up electricity grids across international boundaries and time zones so that countries with different peak periods could exchange power and all of them could reduce their base-load generating capacity. To a limited extent, this is already happening. But a great deal of electricity is also inescapably lost merely in the process of transmitting it (a point dealt with in greater detail later in this chapter) and that imposes limits on the distances over which electricity can be transmitted economically. If we had super-conducting materials which did not drain electricity as it passes through them, we could store it in closed circuits as well as reduce transmission losses and aim for worldwide power exchanges. This is one of the many reasons why research into such materials is now being pursued so vigorously. However, that work still has a very long way to go.

The effects of electricity generation on the environment, on top of any due merely to waste heat, are best illustrated by comparing the quantities of waste which flow annually from different types of 1000MW power stations.

The wastes produced by burning coal for a year in one 1000MW station are in the region of:

1. 7–8 million tonnes of carbon dioxide.
2. 200,000 tonnes of sulphur oxides (dependent on the amount of sulphur in the fuel).
3. 30,000 tonnes of nitrogen oxides.
4. 1000 tonnes of chlorine.
5. 1000 tonnes of heavy metals – zinc, boron, vanadium and arsenic.
7. 250,000 tonnes of ash – fly ash.
8. Significant quantities of radioactive metals and gas (radon) naturally present in coal.

Filtering fly ash out of chimney emissions is relatively cheap and virtually 100 per cent effective. Britain already does it. But control equipment for the sulphur and nitrogen oxides, which respectively cause acid rain and contribute to atmospheric heating and high atmospheric ozone damage, is vastly more expensive. Britain has only just begun to install such equipment and only in a handful of its power stations.

Even control equipment will only recover around 90 per cent of the sulphur and 70 per cent of the nitrogen oxides, and even those oxides which can be contained and removed still have to be put somewhere. A more worrying aspect is that it is not considered possible to prevent the venting into the atmosphere of carbon dioxide and the other substances.

The environmental implications of coal burning are therefore very bleak, and substituting low for high sulphur fuels, as is intended in Britain, is hardly an answer to any of them.

Oil-fired power stations have a slightly happier environmental face. The emissions from a 1000MW oil-fired station lie in the region of:

1. 6–7 million tonnes of carbon dioxide.
2. 84,000 tonnes of sulphur oxides.
3. 28,000 tonnes of nitrogen oxides.
4. 6000 tonnes of ash.

Control equipment eliminates the ash; it could reduce the sulphur and nitrogen oxides by the same percentages as for coal. The problems of cost, disposing of the results, and continued carbon oxide emission are identical.

A 1000MW Natural Gas-fired power station has the cleanest face:

1. 4–5 million tonnes of carbon dioxide.
2. 20 tonnes of sulphur oxides.
3. 25,000 tonnes of nitrogen oxides.
4. 4 tonnes of ash.

As far as nuclear power stations are concerned, obvious considerations of safety make it essential that all radioactive nuclear wastes be contained. Hypothetically at least, nuclear power still has two commanding environmental advantages over all fossil fuels. First, the volume of waste created is physically very small. Quantities are not such that there is no reasonable prospect of containing it, as is the case with burning fossil fuel. Second, fuel does not have to be burned in oxygen in a nuclear power station, so this type of electricity generation does not involve an inevitable and continuing increase in the level of carbon dioxide in the atmosphere. It has been calculated that a nuclear power station saves 99 per cent of the carbon dioxide which would be emitted by a comparable coal-fired station, even allowing for the energy and resources used to build it and produce its fuel.

If our electricity came mostly from nuclear rather than fossil fuels we would not need to worry about the greenhouse effect (see pages 90–91).

But most of our electricity does come from fossil fuel; and there is no prospect of a change to nuclear power in any time-scale that would spare us the environmental consequences of continuing to burn fossil fuel.

One obstacle to substituting nuclear power is political. The quantity of nuclear waste is sufficiently small to make containing it a realistic possibility; but we know that intensely radioactive wastes (the smallest part in volume) must be safely contained for thousands of years. If the Romans had had nuclear power stations, their waste would still have to be safely stored away now. Nuclear scientists are satisfied that it can be done – by casting reprocessed waste in glass and burying it, glassified, in stable layers below the earth. They can point to a natural illustration of the stability of the process: freak geological circumstances caused a half million year-long chain reaction in uranium deposits at Oklo in the Gabon in Africa, and its high-level wastes have not migrated in a billion years. But people do not trust or believe nuclear scientists.

The fear is understandable. We are all haunted by the Russian catastrophe at Chernobyl, and by lesser accidents elsewhere. Nuclear radiation is invisible and inescapably linked in all our minds with cancer, still one of our greatest fears. No amount of lecturing about the inherently dangerous nature of the Chernobyl reactor, the inherently safe nature of other very different reactors, or the safety of waste disposal, is likely to displace such fears. Whatever the arguments for the environmental case, we will not accept them.

The other obstacle is entirely practical. No nation has enough resources to build nuclear-generating capacity sufficient to substitute nuclear for fossil fuel in time; and many developing and third world countries do not have, and could not afford, an electricity distribution network which would allow the use of nuclear power stations, even if they could build them. Widespread use of nuclear power might stave off a fossil fuel-generated environmental catastrophe in our own lifetime, perhaps at the risk of some hazards now and more in the future. But it is too late to think of substituting nuclear for fossil fuels – although it is not too late to think of reducing electricity consumption so that existing nuclear capacity covers more of it.

Details of the waste produced in one year by a 1000MW nuclear power station – note the contrast with that from fossil fuels – complete the picture. The approximate quantities, which vary a little between different types of nuclear reactor, are as follows:

1. 1150 kg of high-level long-life radioactive wastes, requiring long-term containment. After fuel reprocessing and glassification these reduce to a solid 3-metre cube.

2. Between 550 and 1225 cubic metres of medium- to low-level short-life radioactive wastes – gases are usually safely vented to the atmosphere and solids buried in ordinary ground.

Whatever the source of heat from a power station, the amount of waste heat discharged into the environment through cooling towers or in cooling water is about the same. That is an unavoidable component of the high pressure–low pressure differential described earlier. This heat waste can be reduced if the heat can be applied to a useful purpose. Industries such as those described in the first chapter build and operate their own power stations precisely so that they can use both the electrical power and the heat generated. Worldwide, a handful of conveniently located housing estates and horticultural and fish farms also use waste power station heat for space or water heating. But piping and retaining heat in pipes is expensive in terms of cash and resources; piping heat over significant distances can cost more energy than it can save.

People and power stations are seldom good neighbours, and in addition, people seldom live in places where the vast quantities of cooling water required by power stations are found. Most power stations have to be sited well away from large populations and from commercial ventures which could use waste heat. So waste heat is generally an inescapable part of electricity generation.

Turning primary energy into electricity therefore involves losses of heat up the chimney, along with combustion products, and in cooling water; losses of energy from friction as the machinery is driven; losses of electricity required to drive power station pumps and ancillary equipment; and losses from electrical resistance in transmission lines and in the transformers which ultimately reduce transmitted power down to the voltages which we use. The loss from transmission lines turns up in the radio waves which interfere with car radio reception when we drive under them.

As a result of all these inevitable losses, the electricity which finally reaches us reflects at best between 30 and 45 per cent of the energy which went into making it, whatever the source of that energy. The rest, along with combustion products, is waste.

It is for these reasons that several countries – including Britain, until recently – have insisted that fuels such as oil and gas should not be burned in power stations. They are important feed stocks for chemical industries; and a far higher proportion of their energy can be used if they are burned where their energies are needed, as they conveniently can be, to produce heat or drive engines. Unfortunately, burning oil or gas is also the easiest and cheapest way to reduce power station sulphur emissions. As governments snatch at cheap short-term answers to that problem, more oil and gas is likely to be burned to make electricity, not less.

By the time electricity reaches us – the consumers – it is therefore an inherently expensive and wasteful source of heat. Burning it may be less wasteful than burning coal on an open Victorian fire in which all but about 15 per cent of the energy goes up the chimney; but using it as a heat source is far more wasteful than using gas, oil or solid fuel in a modern stove or furnace, which can deliver between 75 and 85 per cent of the fuel's energy for space or water heating or industrial processes. When used in this way, as little as 15 per cent of the energy in the fuel need be wasted – up the chimney but still with its combustion products, of course.

In the home, the moral is quite simple: electricity should only be used when nothing else will reasonably do. We need electricity for electronic equipment such as microwave ovens, radios, televisions, videos, tape-recorders and computers, but electronic equipment only uses very small amounts. We need it for motorised equipment – freezers, vacuum-cleaners, mixers, blenders and refrigerators (though gas refrigerators are also available) – which also require relatively small amounts. We need it for electric lights; and for electric appliances which, while imposing a heavy load while running, compensate for it with their efficiency, convenience and the short time they take to do their job. Thermostatically controlled electric kettles, enclosed cooking and frying pans, and electric irons are examples.

At the domestic level, none of these is a heavy user of electricity. Moreover, modern inventions have made significant inroads into the amount of electricity they need. Fluorescent electric lamps with thin neon or other gas-filled glass elements burn only 17 watts of electricity to produce the same amount of light as the traditional 100-watt tungsten filament bulb. They cost more; but they usually last around 7000 hours against the maximum 1000 hours of most traditional bulbs. Even if such lamps are only fitted in the lighting sockets most regularly used, they will save significant amounts of electricity in any house.

Microwave ovens are another example (though those fitted with a heating element to give food an oven-baked quality use as much energy as comparable ovens heated by gas, electricity or solid fuel). Most rely simply on the microwave process, which uses radio waves in the radar waveband. The radio waves heat food from the inside by agitating the molecules in it, rather than from the outside by heating the whole oven. Microwave ovens are rated at 750 watts or less, and are vastly more economical than the traditional electric oven, rated between 3000 and 5000 watts, or comparable ovens heated by gas, oil or solid fuel.

Electricity is appropriate for these uses; it is not when applied to heating. If gas, oil or solid fuel is used in a modern appliance, the necessary heat can be gained for less than half the quantity of fuel and combustion products involved when electricity is used.

This message may not be welcome to those who generate electricity, nor among those who produce the coal burned to generate most of it. Their only concern is to sell as much coal as possible; and in pursuit of that end they help to maintain the illusion that the efficiency of electricity is comparable to that of other fuels by selling coal to electricity generators at prices far below those at which it is sold for domestic use. In turn, electricity generators further that illusion by offering us cheap rates for off-peak supplies, particularly for space and water heating.

But fuel has to be burned to produce electricity at exactly the same rate and with exactly the same environmental consequences, whatever we pay for it. If we provide a market for excess electricity, we merely encourage complacency in the continued operation of fossil fuel-fired base-load generating capacity at levels well above those desirable in view of the environmental problems that are closing in on us.

Sooner or later, both nationally and worldwide, there will have to be a reduction in the amount of electricity generated unnecessarily; and, along with this, in this amount available at concessionary rates. If we arrange our domestic affairs so that we reduce the number of units of electricity we consume, we will automatically create pressure to reduce the amount of environmental damage to which we contribute with every unit. We will also reduce our exposure to sudden changes in electricity prices.

There has already been a period in the United Kingdom, short-lived admittedly, when electricity producers withdrew part of the off-peak tariff advantage. This left people who had relied on it when they installed off-peak heating and other appliances in a very difficult position. The chances of its happening again, and this time for good, are an inescapable consequence of the waste and environmental damage from which electricity generation cannot be separated. Sooner or later, something will have to be done about excessive base-load generation. It may be an increase in the number of power stations using energies which will bring them to power at a few minutes' notice; it may be a radical increase in the facilities for exchanging power supplies across national boundaries and between different time zones. In these circumstances, it would be unwise for anyone to base long-term plans and investment at home on the assumption that cheap concessionary power will always be available.

Natural and renewable energy

Most people now realise that burning fuel – fossil or nuclear – releases harmful wastes and causes ever-increasing damage to the environment. Too many assume that 'they' can and will soon come up with a kinder alternative; and that in consequence 'we' do not need to do anything about it. Many pin their hopes on energies that are naturally available – solar, wind, wave, tidal, geothermal or water power.

There is a great deal of energy loose in the environment; but three very basic problems apply to most of it. The first is that it is not predictable in quality or quantity; the second is that much of it is not available around the clock; and the third is that most of it is low grade – like sunlight, it is scattered in small quantities all over the place and a great deal has to be collected and concentrated before any significant practical use can be made of it.

Harnessing natural energy presents exactly the same problem as harnessing any energy: how do you get enough energy to create enough pressure at one end of your machine and conditions which allow a sufficient pressure drop at the other? The practical implications emerge when specific natural energy sources are considered.

Wind power

The blades of a windmill or wind turbine (like the wings of a plane) are designed to divide the flow of air over them so that there is a higher pressure ahead than behind – but there must be a flow of air. In addition, the flow has to be fairly constant to be of any use. Making and erecting a wind turbine uses a considerable quantity of energy and resources in itself. If, after erection, it then stands idle for long periods, more energy (and cost) may have been invested in it than can ever be recovered from the electricity it will generate. There are very few sites where wind turbines can ever be economic, either in energy or cash terms. Wherever a wind turbine is built, it should be strong enough to stand occasional winds up to hurricane force; but the investment needed to achieve that strength is soon lost if the average wind flow is 10 mph or less.

Windmills also pose environmental problems. A windmill needs a lot of clear space for an uninterrupted air flow: the wind generating station at Altamont Pass in California, for example, extends over 24 square miles, as against 600–700 acres for a conventional or nuclear power station generating the same power. Large windmills raise a significant sound–pressure wave and would not be tolerable in populated areas.

In any country, these factors combine to limit the amount of energy which can be generated by the wind to a very small proportion of the energy required. Wind power can contribute, but the contribution can only be very small.

As an individual, you might still install a wind generator for your own needs if you thought it made economic or practical sense. (In the United Kingdom you would first have to obtain planning permission to do so.)

Hydro-electric power

Hydro-electric power is most commonly visualised in the schemes already existing worldwide on large rivers. There are, however, very few new places remaining where hydro-electric power can be harnessed on a grand scale; and some existing plants are proving a very poor investment. Not only must there be a large river, and some suitable place where it can be dammed back; the river must also be clean, or silt will rapidly build up behind the dam and frustrate the whole endeavour. This seems to be the likely fate of several grandiose schemes on muddy tropical rivers.

There is very little scope for any significant new hydro-electric scheme in the United Kingdom; but there may be room for many more small private schemes serving individual households which have suitable rivers or streams running through their land. If you are in this fortunate position, you can calculate the theoretical potential with the formula:

$$P = 9.8 \times F \times H kW \text{ (kilowatts)}$$

P (kilowatts) is the power theoretically available; F is the rate of flow in cubic metres per second; and H is the vertical height in metres through which you can design the flow to fall. The actual power potential will be less than the theoretical because of friction and other generating losses.

In the United Kingdom, private schemes require both planning permission and permission from the appropriate local water authority, even if the watercourse you plan to use runs only on your own land. Water authorities have the right to say yes or no to any use or diversion of watercourses, and may also charge for the privilege.

Wave power

Wave power is not something any of us is likely to consider domestically, though the idea might be attractive to someone who owns land on a shoreline regularly battered by the sea.

The authorities concerned with any wave-power scheme in the United Kingdom are the Crown Estate Commissioners who own and control everything below the high water mark, and the local planning authority who control everything you do above it.

The problems of harnessing wave power however, are, truly formidable. Electricity can only be generated from wave energy by building or anchoring a generator which will not move when swell or waves strike it. The necessary pressure drop depends upon the resistance between wave and generator; if the generator moves, that is the end of the story. As we know, it is difficult enough to build sea walls which will not move, and no one has yet built one which has lasted indefinitely.

There have been several pilot wave experiments. One recently commissioned at Islay in the Inner Hebrides involved the construction of an artificial cave in a sea inlet. It is designed so that the incoming waves will compress air in the 'cave' sufficiently to drive a turbine. This will produce enough electricity to light the lamps in 360 houses.

Frankly, no wave scheme offers much hope of profit in the energy field. The object is to harness the power of the sea, but that power fluctuates from flat calm to the massive destructive force of full-scale storms. Even off-shore oil rigs sometimes fail the test, despite all the structural investment which their potential profit allows. In December 1988 an exceptional storm ripped one wave energy plant right off the cliff face to which it was anchored at Bergen in Norway, causing its owners to abandon wave energy. Their experience is unlikely to be unique.

Tidal barrages

Tidal barrages occupy the third limb in modern thought about water power generation. These quite clearly involve construction and investment way beyond the contemplation of any invidual household. In 1965, the French completed a tidal barrage at La Rance in Brittany. It is still the only tidal barrage in the world to make a significant contribution to a national electricity grid. La Rance was conceived as a prototype for a far large project across the bay of Saint Michel. The experience gained convinced the French that it was unwise to proceed with the main scheme.

Britain has long considered the possibility of such schemes, particularly in the Severn estuary which experiences some of the largest tidal ranges in the world, but the problems with the Severn scheme illustrate why tidal energy can at best make only a minor and long delayed contribution to total energy needs.

The Severn tidal range is partly the product of resonances set up by the shape of the estuary. By changing the shape of that estuary, a barrage could on its own lose a metre or more off the range. The rivers which empty into the estuary carry silt which is currently dissipated by the tides, but a build-up of silt behind any barrage could mean the loss of another metre or so. The cost of such a barrage, both in materials and energy, would be significant: an engineer once suggested that it would require more hardcore than is readily available throughout the United Kingdom.

If nothing went wrong a Severn Barrage might cost £8280 million (1989 estimate) and generate 8000MW – 7 per cent of Britain's electricity. At that price, its electricity would cost less than that from the Sizewell pressurised-water nuclear station currently being built, but several times more than that from any conventional power station. Against that, the generating capacity of conventional and nuclear power stations can be calculated with precision in advance; that of the Severn barrage cannot. And Channel Tunnel experience suggests that barrage construction is likely to incur an overrun in costs approaching that of Britain's nuclear programme – a field in which Britain admittedly has an almost unique record. A bill authorising a Mersey barrage which would generate 700MW (0.65 per cent of British electricity) at an initial estimate of £880 million may go ahead in 1991. Work would start in 1995, and be completed in 1999. If the Mersey scheme was successful, a Severn barrage might then proceed.

The unknowns, which now also include the risk of unpredictable rises in sea levels, make estuarial generating schemes highly speculative, with the real possibility that they might not even return the energy and other resources invested in them. Moreover, against that speculation there is a certain environmental loss. Estuaries are an important part of the environment vital to the survival of many wild species, particularly wading and migrant aquatic birds. Their mud flats and marshes would be flooded beyond reach behind barrages.

Solar energy

Solar energy is a favoured natural, renewable and environmentally benign energy option. There is a great deal of solar energy about, but it is very thinly spread. Again, there is the basic problem of how to concentrate it into usable form and whether the end result will redeem the cost of harnessing it. A magnifying glass will concentrate the rays of the sun which pass through it into a pin-point, and raise enough heat to set fire to a piece of paper. The French, following this principle, built an experimental solar furnace, and used mirrors to focus the sunlight falling across a whole valley on to one point. These two examples illustrate the fact that any possible use of solar energy is restricted by the area over which it can reasonably be collected.

The maximum which can be gained from the sun depends on how far one is from the equator. In the latitudes of the United Kingdom, that maximum is about 1.5 kilowatts per square metre. So in ideal conditions (and those exclude night-time, cloudy weather and spring, autumn and winter), one would need to concentrate all the solar energy which falls on 670 square kilometres merely to recover heat equivalent to the output of one ordinary 1000MW nuclear or conventional power station. One would need more (because of generating heat losses) to generate their electrical output.

Solar cells, which convert sunlight directly into electricity, may convert it more efficiently. But they too only yield power equivalent to that collected.

Solar energy is essential to the life of most plants. Trees, and fossil fuels, are in energy terms no more than solar energy which has been collected and stored. We can process plant life into fuel, even burn it directly; but plants too only collect the energy which is there. We would need vast quantities grown over vast areas and competing with food production to substitute plant life for conventional fuels.

Used directly, therefore, solar power is not even in the running as far as large-scale energy generation is concerned.

That is not to say that solar energy cannot contribute at the domestic level. Complex systems for storing solar energy all year round may cost more, both in energy and cash, than any energy recovered will save; but simple systems looped into domestic hot water supplies may be economic in both senses. Attempting to collect enough solar energy to make any meaningful difference all year round is not practical. There would need to be sufficient collectors to pick up worthwhile quantity of energy on clear days in winter; but these would collect so much more in summer that few if any households could use it all. However, a system designed to collect enough between mid-April and mid-September would make some contribution, whatever the weather, and might produce enough to meet the needs of any average household during clear sunny periods.

Between times, of course, only conventional alternatives remain. If your house has a conventional gas, oil or solid fuel boiler for hot water in winter months, you might be able to rely on solar-heated water, topped up with the occasional use of an electric water heater, in the late spring, summer and early autumn – if the weather was fine.

The main problem with domestic solar panel installations is the wide gap between their cost and the value of the energy and environmental economies they will achieve. The price of some commercial installations is such that years may elapse before you redeem your investment with energy saved – if you ever do. If you are able to design and fit your own installation using generally available components the energy equations will be the same, but the economics may be very much better.

Solar heat may be useful if you have a swimming pool, not least because the large quantity of water in the pool will act as a reservoir for the heat you put into it. But swimming pools themselves do nothing to help the environment.

Heat pumps

It may be worth considering heat pumps for water heating, whether they draw their energy from solar-heated water (or indeed any water), an area of soil or the air. Essentially, a heat pump reverses the principle of the refrigerator: it collects heat by circulating a gas through pipes run in water, soil or air, and then compresses the gas so as to release that heat in concentrated form, typically into a hot-water system. The amount of heat produced may be two, three or more times the heat represented by the electricity used to drive it, depending on whether the source is air, soil or liquid and how hot the source is. So a heat pump may redeem the energy lost in producing the electricity which drives it. But heat pump installations are expensive. Most have only proved economic in commercial uses. For example, dairy farmers who have to cool large quantities of milk and also need plenty of hot water in the dairy have found that a heat pump does both jobs for them profitably.

Methane

The production of methane from sewage or farm and other slurries or wastes is another of the naturally renewable energy options under general consideration. The process is well established in sewage treatment and many sewage works are driven by the gas which they generate.

The principle of methane production is simple: if organic matter decays in water or any other place where it is deprived of oxygen, naturally occuring bacteria break that matter down, giving off methane and carbon dioxide as they do so. Both are gases which retain heat in the earth's atmosphere and contribute to the greenhouse effect, but methane retains 30 times more heat than carbon dioxide. Collecting and burning methane is therefore preferable to releasing it, even though carbon dioxide is produced when it is burned.

The possibility of recovering methane from refuse tips is under consideration, and some farms and other commercial undertakings use anaerobic digestion of their slurries and wastes to yield gas which can be burned or will drive a static combustion engine, and to break down organic wastes so that they are easier to use and are not as foul-smelling. The ordinary domestic septic tank also relies on anaerobic digestion for its efficient functioning.

Methane from sources such as these could in due course make some small contribution to overall energy needs; this may be necessary as part of general measures to protect the environment from excessive methane releases. Again, however, the contribution is not likely to be significant.

It may be experimentally interesting to try and produce methane domestically, but will almost certainly be expensive and unprofitable. The volume of organic waste available in any ordinary household is not sufficient to generate significant quantities of the gas. The costs include: containing those wastes within a suitable vessel; keeping them stirred so that it does not clog up; insulating the vessel to maintain temperatures which best favour the reaction; piping and storing the gas safely (it is the same gas as that recovered in oil drilling and is explosive); and cleaning out the carbon dioxide, which forms with it and is not combustible. Those costs combine to challenge the value of any advantage which might be sought on the domestic scale.

Geothermal energy

Geothermal energy is the last of the supposedly environmentally friendly energy options under general consideration. Again, the theory is simple: some areas have hot rock underneath them; if there are no usable hot geysers already spouting from them, you drill down into the rock, pump water into it, and use the steam which boils back to drive a turbine. Radioactive decay in rocks such as granite is often responsible for the heat, and the principle has been explored experimentally in the United Kingdom in Cornwall, where such conditions exist. However, the quantity of heat which can be gained, and the technical difficulty of ensuring that the source continues to deliver despite water being pumped through it, combine to defeat any prospect of significant geothermal energy supplies.

Conclusion

Only one conclusion remains at the end of the day: if we go on burning energy at present rates virtually all of it will come from coal, oil, natural gas or nuclear power. Producers of that power may be compelled – at increasing cost to us – to clean up their act by scrubbing ash, sulphur and nitrogen oxides out of power station chimneys. But if this is this case, the result will be mountains of those recovered substances – and something has to be done with those mountains. They have to go back into the environment somewhere as there is nowhere else to put them.

The facts are simple. All uses of energy will result in further corruption of the environment. The only way to minimise that corruption is to reduce the amount of energy we use. It is up to each and every one of us to contribute.

3

Home Energy Use

This chapter pursues the principles of the previous chapter into the details of home life. We waste energy at home in many ways. We let heat leak out and cold leak in; we make inefficient use of appliances driven by energy; and we use appliances which are more wasteful than existing alternatives.

Thermal insulation

Adequate insulation is the obvious answer to heat loss. In theory a candle would suffice to warm a room which was perfectly insulated, and even that would hardly be necessary since each of us gives off around 500 watts of heat all the time – the equal of a single bar of an electric fire. That is why heat builds up so rapidly in crowded rooms.

Very few houses come anywhere near a state of perfect insulation; and while we can now build new ones which do, the resource and energy cost of scrapping all existing houses and replacing them would be vastly greater than the amount that could be saved. We have to do the best with what we have.

Preventing heat losses involves more than insulation, but it is a good place to begin before moving on to look at the wider field.

Insulation

Heat rises, so the first concern must be to stop it rising out of our roofs and into the open air. If the space above upper ceilings is accessible, that is fairly simple: merely lay 7 mm or more of fibreglass, other mineral wool or insulating granules (the thicker the better) between the rafters. The only essential precaution is to ensure that all water-pipes and other water apparatus are below the insulation, on our side of it. If not they could freeze and burst in cold weather.

If upper ceilings are fitted directly to the underside of the rafters, as they are in many older houses, it may be impossible to obtain access to install insulation without tearing out ceilings or relaying the roof. If either of these is necessary, fixing an insulating material between the rafters before the roof or ceiling is reformed will help as long as the slates are laid on bituminous felt, or there is some other barrier to keep the wind out. Otherwise, spraying the underside of the slates with one of the proprietary materials now available for both fixing slates and insulating is likely to be the best bet. Insulation will not make much difference if the wind can blow through it.

If a roof or ceiling does not have to be moved, some advantage can be still be gained by lining the underside of the ceiling with an appropriate insulation board and redecorating over it. If you are lucky enough to have a thatched roof, the roof itself will solve your insulation problems. Thatch, like a tea-cosy, is inherently heat retentive.

Walls and ground floors are the next problem. If you have cavity walls, the answer is to have the cavities pressure filled with one of the proprietary insulators available. If your ground floors have to be rebuilt, an insulating barrier can be included when they are reformed. Otherwise, there is not a great deal anyone can do except to insulate the inside of the room. Carpets and other floor coverings perform quite adequately with floors, as they have done for centuries. Constructing false internal walls on existing walls, with an insulator or insulating air space between the two, is an expensive solution to the wall problem. Ordinary wall coverings, from the ancient method of hanging tapestry onwards, all help.

Lagging hot-water cylinders is the other basic insulation imperative – unless you want yours to double as an expensive and inefficient radiator. The same goes also for any long runs of pipework which carry hot water. Cheap proprietary hot-water cylinder jackets are generally available and are stocked at most electricity board showrooms in the United Kingdom; and most builder's merchants supply foam plastic pipe-insulation tubes which are easy to fit.

Insulation does not – or should not – end with the structural components of houses. We can easily insulate ourselves by wearing a few more clothes. The modern move towards houses heated throughout to almost sub-tropical temperatures is inordinately wasteful of energy. Except for some elderly people and those at risk from hypothermia, this level of heat does us more harm than good. It may be comfortable to have houses which are so warm that we can wander around stark naked if we wish, but it is hardly necessary. More clothes, less heat, and fewer heated rooms would not hurt us, and would do a power of good to the environment.

Draught exclusion

Other aspects of heat retention involve keeping cold out rather than keeping warmth in. If window-frames are not airtight, cold air blows in and we have to burn more energy to achieve a given level of comfort. Double-glazing is an expensive answer to the problem, though it may cost less than total replacement of window-frames with new airtight ones. If window-frames are already airtight, the cost of double-glazing in energy and resources saved is not likely to be redeemed. Heat loss through glass alone is relatively small: thick blinds or curtains which prevent warm internal air flowing across cold glass surfaces can save as much as double-glazing, particularly if they are left drawn through the night when the coldest external conditions usually occur. Most of us already have curtains.

In every house, external doors pose the other basic heat-retention problem. Part of that problem remains even if the doors themselves are entirely wind-and airtight. If they open directly into internal living areas, you exchange your expensive warm air for abundant external cold air every time they are opened.

There is nothing to beat the traditional porch as an answer to the door problem. Porches are either built outside an external door or enclose a small lobby within it. As long as the outer and inner doors are not open at the same time, a porch operates as an air lock, preventing cold air from rushing into a house and severely restricting the heat which can travel the other way when the outer door is open.

You need planning permission before you can build a porch outside your house if the porch does not fall within the limits laid down by the Town & Country Planning (General Development) Order 1988. If an external porch will cover more than 3 square metres of ground, or any part of it will exceed 3 metres in height or be within 2 metres of a boundary fronting a highway, permission must be obtained to build it. But no permission is needed to partition off a porch within a house. Many older houses, built with a passageway leading back from the front door, include such porches as a standard feature.

Draught exclusion problems
If you heat your house by burning a combustible fuel – oil, gas or solid fuel – the combustion process consumes air in the house and pumps it up the chimney or flue along with fuel combustion wastes. As a result, any burner constantly sucks cold air into your house through any space through which it will flow. If you achieved the impossible and made your house completely airtight, the burner would not function properly. Among other hazards, you might then face the risk of poisonous carbon monoxide fumes leaking back into your house. That risk can arise even if you are partially successful and have a less than adequate air flow.

If you have a fuel-burning appliance which requires an air flow you can greatly reduce the risk of unwelcome cold breezes flowing through areas of your house where they are not wanted. If you connect an air-pipe from some place outside the house (that includes a ventilated under-floor area if you have hollow ground floors) to a point nearest to the burner, the combustion process will draw the air it needs in through the pipe and straight into the burner. A pipe of around 5 cm diameter will usually suffice, but the higher the level of draught proofing in a house, the greater the volume of air drawn through it will be. Such a pipe will reduce flows of cold air everywhere else. It may eliminate them altogether.

Unfortunately, nothing in life is ever entirely simple. If you succeed in stopping all draughts through your house and achieve optimal energy conservation as a result, you may then begin to have trouble with condensation and mildew in corners where air is stagnant. Water vapour is present in every house: apart from emitting heat, we all emit water vapour and so also do virtually all our cooking and other operations.

Condensation, and the mildew which it encourages, can often be cured simply by opening windows and making sure that there is a good flow of air when external conditions are warm. It can be tackled mechanically by installing an electric dehumidifier (which may be desirable anyway in areas of high natural humidity). In many cases the energy and resources used by a dehumidifier will be less than those lost by heating a house through which the air rushes doing the job naturally. If mildew does develop it can be swiftly removed from any painted, emulsioned or other surface which will not discolour by wiping with undiluted domestic bleach. This is one of the few instances where bleach used in the home should not cause harm to the environment – provided that the cloth is not rinsed out down the drain afterwards.

A far more serious risk is attached to unthinking efforts to eliminate draughts. Conditions may arise which encourage wet or dry rot to develop in timber. Never try to reduce draughts by blocking air bricks or other apertures which ventilate areas under your ground floors; they must be kept clear even at the price of draughts. And make sure that nothing is ever placed or left against the external walls of your house above any damp course. That will merely encourage damp to spread into the fabric with consequences which will be costly to remedy in terms both of cash and resources.

Appliances

As far as appliances are concerned, few of us are very good at keeping pace with modern developments, or for that matter at weighing up the energy efficiency of appliances when we choose them. With all that has been written in the previous chapter it hardly needs emphasising that high-efficiency oil, gas or solid fuel appliances are desirable permanent fixtures for space and water heating. But what about the rest? All electrical appliances have their wattage stamped on them somewhere so their impact can be judged. Add up the total wattage of the appliances you are running: every 1000 watts run for an hour costs you and the environment one unit of electricity.

Lighting

Lighting involves the most constantly insidious use of energy in any house. One light bulb uses very little energy, but very few of us now manage with only one at a time. Ten 60-watt bulbs consume more electricity than a single bar of an electric fire. Many of us use at least that number (or their equivalent in higher-powered lamps) for long hours in the day. Switching off all unnecessary lights is an obvious partial solution; but only a fanatical energy saver is likely to do that habitually, and anyway some lamps have to stay on. The answer is to fit lamps which produce the same amount of light for less power.

Long neon tubes were the original option in this field. It takes heat to produce the light of a conventional light bulb – the white heat of a hard tungsten metal element – and using electricity to produce heat is inherently wasteful. Neon tube light is radiated by the gas inside the tube which fluoresces (shines) when a relatively low electric current is passed through it. However, the light produced by long neon tubes can seem a little stark at home.

The neon tube principle has now been successfully incorporated into lamps not much different in shape and size from the ordinary light bulb, which can be fitted into standard light-bulb fittings. Typically, such lamps draw 17 watts of electricity for the same amount of light as is produced by a conventional 100-watt light bulb. They are more expensive, of course; but the additional cost is repaid by lower electricity consumption and by the fact that such lamps may last 7000 hours or more against the 1000-hour standard of the ordinary light bulb. Even if they are only installed in the light fittings most commonly in use, a householder who fits such lamps can achieve a measurable reduction in electricity used without further thought.

Refrigerators and freezers

Refrigerators and freezers are switched on all the time and virtually ignored once installed. Both play an important part in saving other resources. They help to save waste of perishable foods, and make it possible to grow or buy many foods in bulk and reduce the number of energy-consuming journeys which have to be made to suppliers.

A fridge or freezer will not add much to the electricity consumed by an ordinary household, but the total number in use adds significantly to overall electricity consumption. There are more than 30 million fridges and freezers in British households. Together, they burn over 2000 megawatts of electricity – equal to the output of two large power stations. Much of that is unnecessarily wasted. On average, existing cooling equipment uses between 2 and 3kWh (units) of electricity a year for each litre of space in it; better design can reduce that to figures as low as 0.2–0.4kWh per litre. So it is important to enquire about running costs when any new fridge or freezer is purchased.

However well or wastefully refrigerators and freezers are designed, the way they are used and the basic design chosen make important differences to additional wastage.

Virtually all are now thermostatically controlled. Though switched on all the time, they only run and consume energy when the temperature within them rises above the level at which they are set. Saving energy used by cooling equipment is therefore also a matter of reducing to a minimum the number of occasions when that happens.

All cooling equipment warms up and needs more energy to cool down again when it comes into contact with the outside air, so it is important to keep the door of a fridge or freezer closed as far as possible.

Less obvious is the waste which occurs when ice is allowed build up around the cooling elements in a refrigerator, and over those buried in the walls of a freezer. Ice is a very good insulator – a fact discovered thousands of years ago by Eskimos when they first built igloos. A layer of ice between the inside of a fridge or freezer and its cooling elements swiftly reduces the amount of heat which those elements can draw out. When the elements are covered by ice and the internal temperature rises, the thermostat cuts in as it usually does; but the equipment then burns up unnecessary energy as it tries to draw enough heat out through the insulating ice for the temperature to drop back below the level at which the thermostat is set. We save energy if we defrost our appliances regularly, as manufacturers advise us.

Domestic refrigerators have a low energy rating and do not add much to the energy costs of individual households. They are not intended to do any more than cool their contents. Indeed, people who live in old houses with larders designed for the days before refrigeration may still manage without them. Freezers are a very different matter.

The most popular freezer is now the upright variety with hung doors which swing on vertical hinges like a house door. They are convenient because it is easy to see what is on the shelves; but they are very wasteful of energy.

Hot air rises and cold air falls; so every time the door of upright freezer is opened, most of its expensively produced cold air falls out and energy has to be burned to replace it. You may need a good memory or marking system to find your stores in a chest freezer, with a door which opens horizontally at the top, but as far as energy conservation is concerned such freezers are a much better bet. Most of the cold air stays locked in the chest even when it is opened.

It used to be fairly easy to obtain very large chest freezers with a capacity of 20 cubic feet (0.56 cubic metres) or more, but public taste favoured smaller upright freezers and manufacturers have responded to it: large chest freezers are less easy to find nowadays.

This is unfortunate for energy conservation. The manufacture of large freezers does not require significantly more resources than that of small ones; and very little more energy is needed to run a large freezer, though energy use is always more efficient if freezers are kept fairly full. If you only have space for a small upright freezer, there is little you can do about it. But if you have space, consider investing in a large chest freezer if you do not already have one.

Even small families can keep a large freezer full as long as they do not use it merely as a convenient parking lot for pre-packed frozen foods from a local freezer centre; and, properly used, a large chest freezer can become the cornerstone of a household's efforts to reduce use of energy and other resources.

With a large freezer you can bulk buy (or make) and freeze bread, and (particularly if you have a microwave oven to thaw it out) have fresh bread whenever you want without having to make a special journey to buy it. You can bulk buy (or maybe produce) meat, fish, fruit and vegetables – freezing what is not immediately required, thus saving journeys and cost.

If you produce fruit or vegetables in your garden, you can schedule your whole crop for the best growing season (no more successional sowing) and freeze the surplus for year-round use.

You can cook food in large quantities far more economically in terms of cost and resources than if the same amount is cooked in small quantities. The food not required for immediate consumption can be frozen in portions convenient for later use. You know what has gone into the convenience foods you make and freeze yourself; and you know that if you freeze them freshly they will not be contaminated by bacteria. You do not know what has happened to commercially produced convenience foods along the way from original preparation to shop shelf. Laws and procedures designed to protect you may not compensate for illness, even death, if they fail.

You can also preserve parts of foods which would otherwise go to waste, such as bones, meat and vegetable scraps, by boiling them up for stock and freezing it for later use in soups and casseroles. Stock can be frozen in some of those otherwise wasted plastic boxes used to package so many items these days. A good supply of stock is an essential part of any good cook's armoury. With an adequate freezer you do not need to depend on the traditional, constantly bubbling stock cauldron still found in some of the best and biggest restaurant kitchens; or face the additional expense (in cash and resources) of the standard flavour stock cubes we all buy for convenience.

Cooking appliances

Many modern appliances use resources, and cook, far more efficiently and conveniently than the traditional alternatives with which most of us grew up. In the kitchen, the open hot plate, hob or gas ring and the conventional oven have been central to the experience of many of us. But heating anything on an open ring is inherently wasteful because so much heat escapes up past the pan on it; and heating anything in a pan without a lid on is even more wasteful, as the heat then escapes out of the pan as well.

Heating a whole oven in order to heat its contents – and drawing on anything between 3000 and 5000 watts of electricity or the gas or other equivalent – is vastly more wasteful than merely heating the food, as with a microwave oven drawing perhaps 750 watts. In addition, microwave cooking preserves more of the food's nutritional value and flavour. Faster cooking and the need for far less cooking water account for the difference.

We can do better, and be kinder to the environment, with modern equipment. Thermostatically controlled electric kettles and enclosed cooking and deep frying pans with built-in electric elements deliver only as much heat as is needed and only where it is needed. They also keep it there, often along with with cooking smells which might otherwise be troublesome.

By using the higher temperature and penetrating power of steam to do what boiling water does in an ordinary pan, pressure cookers tackle the open cooking ring job more efficiently.

With a little thought, many households could now manage virtually all their cooking with an electric kettle, a couple of cooking pans, perhaps an electric toaster or grill for occasional use, and a microwave oven – and do it far more efficiently in every sense of the word. This is particularly true for small household consisting of only one or two people. Such households are now the majority in the United Kingdom.

Vacuum-cleaners and electric irons

Some appliances are apparently paradoxical: high-powered versions may be more efficient than low-powered alternatives. Vacuum-cleaners and electric ironing equipment come into this category.

The suction power of a vacuum-cleaner is directly related to the power of the motor which drives the fan inside it; so too is the probable life of that motor. A vacuum-cleaner with a 1000-watt motor used in moderation is likely to last longer and to pick up dust far more quickly than one with a 250-watt motor which is over-stretched. The low-powered one may use more energy and resources than the more powerful one, both in day-to-day running and overall.

Conventional electric irons contrast similarly with motorised rotary irons, usually controlled by a pedal. A conventional iron is generally rated at 1000 watts, a rotary one at 1200. But it is much quicker to do the job with a rotary iron, once you realise that shirts and similar garments are still essentially flat if unbuttoned and ironed that way. The shorter running time saves the extra energy needed to drive the rotary iron. The larger area of a rotary iron's heat element, usually significantly greater than that of a flat iron, also saves wear on clothes. The heat is more widely distributed and, the whole operation also saves wear and tear on the operator. Ironing is quicker, and the blade pressure of a typical rotary iron comes from the pedal, not from the bent back of the operator leaning over it.

Automatic washing-machines

The automatic washing-machine can probably be singled out as the most environmentally friendly of all household appliances. It washes clothes more efficiently than most people could hope to do by any traditional method, uses little if any more water than those methods would require, and allows thorough, energy-saving, low-temperature washing. The latter is probably beyond the scope of any traditional washing method, except perhaps that of beating clothes clean against a rock in a river. Centrifugal spin-drying, virtually standard in all modern washing-machines, is far and away the most efficient way of extracting water from wet clothes; it saves drying time and resources if clothes have to dried with a heated drier.

Dishwashers and electric tumbler-driers

Automatic dishwashers and electric tumbler-driers stand at the opposite end of the environmental scale to the clothes washing-machine. The amount of electricity and water used by dishwashers varies between models and with the washing programme chosen: they are generally rated at between 2500 and 3500 watts and the full washing cycle may consume between

25 and 35 litres of water. You only need six litres of water to fill an average plastic washing-up bowl; and if you wash the dishes in one with water at a comfortable temperature and rinse in another with water as hot as you can manage, everything will dry germ, stain and detergent free almost immediately it is placed in a dishrack. Even if you have a dishwasher you will spend time stacking and unstacking, and you will have to wash oven dishes and similar utensils by hand. Manual washing-up need not take any longer, and the environment benefits all round.

The electric tumbler-drier is a menace because, like all electric heating appliances, it burns a great deal of energy very quickly. Three thousand watts is a fairly typical rating. Tumbler-driers may be convenient in emergencies or for short-lived special uses, but it does not make much sense either to the environment or to any domestic economy to invest in them just for the odd occasion. People who believe they are helping the environment by using washable babies' nappies rather than disposable ones defeat their own objectives if they dry them in a tumbler-drier. Drying clothes is one operation to which wind and solar power really can be harnessed easily with the aid of either a rack or washing-line. Tumbler-driers should not be treated as an appropriate substitute.

Minor appliances

There are many minor electrical appliances more convenient than their manual alternatives, among them hair-driers and electric razors, carving-knives, mixers, blenders, toothbrushes, curling tongs and so on. None of them uses much electricity; all may save labour, but their production and use still involves extra resources. So a purist would say, use the labour and do without them.

Electronic equipment

The last group of household appliances is the electronic group, which includes radios, televisions, audio equipment, computers, videos-recorders and clocks. Resources are consumed and waste is generated in manufacturing all of these, of course; but the amount of energy needed to run them has fallen to almost negligible proportions since transistors and micro-circuitry came on the scene.

However, this only remains true if they are powered from a mains electricity supply. Batteries are costly in terms of cash, resources and waste. Many, particularly sealed rechargeable batteries, include highly toxic heavy metals such as cadmium which add just a little more to environmental pollution each time they are manufactured or disposed of. Even appliances which do not have a built-in mains lead usually have a plug connection for a transformer lead; and multi-connecting transformers which cost little more than a couple of battery replacements are available, so a transformer soon pays for itself. Wherever possible, therefore, any electronic appliance which is only powered by a battery should be avoided.

Motor vehicles

Most of us use cars or other motorised vehicles to bridge at least some of the gaps which separate our domestic lives from the outside world. Vehicles head the list of desirable possessions which damage the environment. Apart from our homes, our cars cost more, and more to run – in cash, resources and pollution – than anything else we individually own or do.

Burning lead-free petrol saves the environment from unwanted lead, but it does not spare the damage caused by winning oil, processing it into fuel, and burning that fuel. If catalytic converters were installed in every car's exhaust they would not eliminate anything like all the carbon and nitrogen oxides emitted by internal combustion engines. And a long time will elapse before there is any technical improvement. In 1990, Britain's Transport Secretary predicted that there would be no significant reduction in vehicle carbon dioxide emissions before the year 2010. Vehicle engines contribute as much as one-fifth of all Britain's carbon dioxide emissions.

In the lower atmosphere, car exhaust emissions add to the constituents of acid rain and to the damage it causes to plant life and buildings. Unburned fuel and oil and petroleum combustion products contribute to the rising incidence of cancer. Carbon and nitrogen oxides fuel the greenhouse effect. The sun's ultra-violet light reacts with vehicle exhaust gases causing complex chemical reactions which result in the formation of toxic ground-level ozone. In still, sunny weather in heavily polluted urban atmospheres, that ozone accumulates above the tiny levels which even healthy people can tolerate. Ozone also adds to the greenhouse effect.

Car exhaust emissions migrate into the upper atmosphere and there, along with other man-made pollutants, they contribute to the destruction of ozone. We rely on ozone in the upper atmosphere to shield us from excessive ultra-violet radiation (see pages 91–3). We can only stand infinitesimally small doses of it in the air we breathe. Our vehicle emissions are helping to defeat all our interests.

The only major improvement which individuals can contribute would be to use their vehicles less, particularly in congested urban areas. But some quite simple things would help a little. The faster we go, the more fuel we burn. The World Wide Fund for Nature has calculated that vehicle fuel consumption would be reduced by as much as 2.4 per cent if road users did no more than observe the British 70 mph speed limit. And cars fitted with radial rather than the less common cross-ply tyres use between 6 and 8 per cent less fuel.

Unfortunately, our passion for the motor car is so deeply entrenched that none of us seems likely to give up using it willingly, even if we have an entirely adequate alternative. Would the message sink in if we were told that within six months our vehicles would carry us, like lemmings, over a cliff of environmental destruction? Would we not convince ourselves even then that what *we* were doing did not matter?

It has not come to that – yet. But the example we set is already critical. Worldwide, billions of people hanker after our way of life. If many of them achieve it, we shall all suffer in the end if we continue to place the private motor car at the apex of that way of life.

One can only write hopefully. In a better world we would walk, cycle, or use public transport wherever possible; we would hire vehicles for short-term special needs, possess only the smallest vehicle consistent with our average needs, use it only when nothing else would do, and then as infrequently as possible and over the shortest possible distance. We would buy cars, if at all, for their lasting qualities, and replace them only when beyond feasible repair. We would so arrange our journeys with friends or neighbours that none of us ever travelled without passengers. Passengers can legally contribute to running costs in the United Kingdom.

Many people are already aware of these facts, but reminders are still necessary. Most of us cause more environmental damage with our cars than we do through any other single activity.

◆ 4 ◆

The Waste We Throw Out

From our homes we throw waste in solid, liquid and gaseous forms back into the environment. Solids usually go into the local authority domestic waste collection, liquids down the drain, and gases from substances burned into the atmosphere.

Gaseous waste

Gases created by the fuels we burn and the ways in which we burn them or contribute to their burning have been discussed in the last two chapters. Their effect in the atmosphere is considered more fully in Chapter 7 on pages 88–93. We can only contribute to their reduction in the ways already discussed: the best thing we can do, therefore, is to burn as little as possible, and consume fewer products which demand the burning of energy.

At the domestic level there is an environmental paradox. These days, most domestic rubbish is collected in plastic bags, carted off and buried in open landfill tips. If food and other organic waste which will slowly rot is included in that solid waste, dogs, cats, rats or foxes (even in towns these days) will often sniff it out before it is collected. They will rip open the bags and scatter everything, adding to the general litter, even while the sacks stand outside in the street awaiting collection.

Even if that does not happen and rubbish reaches the tip intact as intended, anything edible is likely to end up as a welcome addition to the diet of rats and other vermin, encouraging a further increase in their number – which has already reached levels that pose a serious health hazard. For example, it is now dangerous to come into contact, even accidentally, with the water in many canals and other watercourses because it contains the organisms of Weil's disease, spread in rats' urine.

Any food and organic waste which then remains (and large proportions do) will decompose; but because rubbish is buried away from oxygen, the processes of decomposition will release methane along with some carbon dioxide – typically 70 parts of methane for every 30 parts of carbon dioxide. The increase in the general level of methane released is a matter of growing concern because of its contribution to the greenhouse effect (see pages 93–6). Methane retains 30 times more heat than carbon dioxide, so it is important to reduce the amount of organic waste which is tipped.

Part of that reduction can come from using up everything which can be used (dealt with later in this chapter on pages 59–61). But if after that you can compost or burn organic rubbish at home rather than send it to the tip, the environment will benefit. Loose composting or burning will produce carbon dioxide; burying rubbish in landfill sites will produce the far more heat-retentive methane, as well as attracting scavengers and feeding vermin.

This is one case in which the pollution you create and can see for yourself at home may be less harmful than that to which you contribute and cannot see somewhere else.

Your neighbours might not see it that way, of course, particularly if they are saving energy by hanging their washing out to dry when you light your fire. So it pays to be considerate. If you have a solid fuel stove, that could be the best place in which to burn small quantities of rubbish, particularly animal bones. An efficient garden incinerator is better than an open bonfire, for obvious reasons.

Municipal authorities do not burn waste because confining it to landfill sites is a great deal cheaper. Incineration has been explored. Resources could be saved with profit if the energy which waste contains could be used. Each year British authorities collect 25 million tonnes of domestic and commercial waste. Burned, it would yield energy equivalent to 5.5 million tonnes of oil – more than 5 per cent of British oil consumption.

Practical problems prevent the harnessing of that energy. Waste sources are widely scattered and long-distance transport would dissipate their value; raw waste cannot be stored, and the supplies available at individual locations would suffice only to fuel small power stations. They cannot generate electricity economically because of the energy lost in the process and the high cost of generating equipment. Raw waste would produce heating steam at a profit, but to use that steam we would need incinerators in populous residential and commercial areas where every aspect of waste burning is unwelcome. Piping steam is costly and disruptive, and buyers who have existing heating systems are unlikely to invest in new ones. Sheffield is one of the few places in Britain which has such a scheme.

A handful of large local authorities has invested in complex and costly plant which sorts waste and pelletises the combustible part into fuel. Such fuel has 60 per cent of the heat value of power station coal. Pelletised waste could be collected and burned in large power stations if the majority of waste disposal authorities could afford the necessary plant – but the majority cannot afford it.

Solid waste

If you have convenient local disposal facilities into which you can separate wastes such as aluminium cans, glass bottles and paper for recycling, obviously you should aim to use them. Even that requires caution, however: you can easily burn more fuel and resources by driving with supposedly recyclable wastes to a central collection point than will afterwards be saved by recycling them.

Bottle-banks and other general recycling facilities do not exist unless it is economic (in cash and resources) to collect and remove waste sorted and deposited in them. But few of us are equal to the task of calculating whether our end of the exercise makes environmental sense. By and large, if dumping waste in a central collection point involves your making a journey which you would not otherwise make, it won't. All your intended economy will vanish in the resource cost of the journey.

Sorting solid waste for external recycling is only part of the picture. Recycling begins and is at its most efficient at home.

A host of things we buy these days come ready packed in plastic boxes and other containers. All represent manufacturing resources already used by petrochemical and other industries. Cellophane apart, they all take a very long time to decay naturally, and burning them releases several harmful gases. Plastic containers are ideal for storing dry foods in the kitchen and chilled and frozen foods in the refrigerator and freezer: they should be kept for that purpose. It makes no sense at all to throw them away and then buy and use cling-film and plastic containers for the same job – which requires additional resources and involves further environmental harm.

Cartons in which cream, yoghurt and similar substances are sold are useful for plants. Punch a small drainage hole in the bottom and you have an ideal substitute for the flower-pot or seedling container. Many gardeners already use them instead of the tailor-made plastic or ceramic alternatives, which again swallow up additional resources.

ICI has recently announced the first commercial use of a plastic, Biopol, developed from fermented organic sugars rather than the oil by-products which make up most other plastics. Biopol decomposes completely in soil bacteria when tipped and buried. Decomposition releases carbon dioxide; but this is balanced by the carbon dioxide taken up naturally to produce the sugars. So once Biopol and plastics like it are in general use, dumping them will not contribute to the build-up of plastic litter or carbon dioxide. At present, however, Biopol costs 40 times more than conventional plastics; and though ICI estimate that large-scale production will eventually reduce that to three times the normal cost, this extra cost alone is likely to ensure that ordinary plastics will be with us for a long time to come unless someone forces the manufacturer's hand. If this happens we will pay more for packaging.

Packaging is so basic to the marketing of manufactured goods that whatever happens in the future all of us are still likely to be left with some glass, metal, plastic, paper and carboard rubbish or containers which we can only burn or throw out. But with a little thought we can all reduce their quantity and by doing that, the additional resources used to provide alternatives. Everything helps, from buying loose rather than prepacked goods to making sure that we re-use the ubiquitous plastic carrier bag rather than accept yet another.

Food wastes

Food wastes are residues of something which has already cost an arm and a leg in resource terms when we buy it. In the days when some beef cattle were reared exclusively on barley, for example, seven tonnes of barley feed went into producing every tonne of beef. All the animal protein we consume and waste – fish, meat, eggs, milk and their products – involves a similarly profligate conversion of foods and resources. We should therefore recover for our own consumption all we possibly can.

Nowadays, something as simple as the declining use of home made cooking stock contributes significantly to food waste. After we have consumed all the meat we want we can further reduce the waste inherent in what is left by boiling bones or poultry carcases in a pan or pressure cooker and preserving or freezing the resulting stock – in some of those plastic boxes. Some vegetable wastes can also be dealt with in this way.

When we have recovered all we can, our pets may be able to recover more from what is left, saving at least part of the formidable resources swallowed up by the pet-food industry; and though there may then be no choice but to burn or put out for the domestic waste collection any animal residues which remain, virtually all vegetable residues can be composted for use in the garden. Even tea leaves are useful there, particularly for improving soils in which herbs are grown, including soils in window-boxes.

As individuals, we can probably recycle more of our own waste than public services can. There may be a limit to what anyone living in a flat in a tower block can do; but everyone can do something, and many of us could do a great deal more than we do. If we reduced the volume of solid waste which leaves our homes, and reduced the proportion of it which can cause further harm, we would be contributing to the advantage of the environment. The ideal rubbish bag is one which contains at most inert substances – ashes, cans, bottles and containers which may rust but will not rot.

Liquid wastes

Similar principles apply to the liquid wastes we generate and then flush down the drain. The quantity of liquid waste we release relates very closely to the amount of fresh water we use.

The British Water Authorities Association calculates that on average each of us uses 125 litres of water (28 gallons) a day. The largest part of it is flushed down the loo – between 35 and 39 litres per person every day. Dish-washing and cleaning (28 to 32 litres) and bathing and showering (18 to 21 litres) come next, though baths generally use more water than showers. We only use between 10 and 13 litres as drinking and cooking water.

The quantity matters both because it costs energy and re-sources to pipe clean water into our homes in the first place; and because it costs still more to treat it after we have fouled it and sent it on its way.

But the quality of the waste water we release is particularly important. If we put environmentally harmful substances into water when we use it, it may be impossible to remove them during subsequent treatment, and is in any event costly in resources. We increase the volume of harmful residues which flows into the general environment every time we add harmful substances to our water.

Quantities

As far as the quantity of water we use is concerned, nothing concentrates the mind more than having to pay for your water through a water meter. However, very few houses in the United Kingdom are yet supplied through meters. If you are concerned for the environment you will not wait until yours is.

Obviously, dripping taps and leaking pipes are to be avoided; so too are dishwaters (which have already been reviewed on page 52). Many of us have ingrained habits which are wasteful, such as washing-up under running taps, or washing anything up or away in small quantities when a short delay will allow the same quantity of water to be used for a larger job. Fastidious people may not enjoy the thought of not flushing the loo every time it is used, or of allowing washing or washing-up to pile up before tackling them. But most of the pure water we consume is used for these purposes.

We can also save loo water systematically. The cisterns on most loos hold a good deal more water than is usually needed to flush them; cisterns empty and are refilled every time they are flushed. During Britain's 1976 drought the Duke of Edinburgh suggested that everyone should lift the lid off the loo cistern and put a brick in it, saving water equal to the volume of the brick with each flush. You can achieve the same result, with less risk to the cistern and its equipment, by filling a suitable plastic bottle – recycled of course – with water and sinking it in the cistern. If you do this your water saving is regular, permanent, effortless and considerable.

It also helps significantly if you can avoid the use of top-quality drinking water for purposes which do not require it. That too is not difficult. The rain falls on all of us, and can provide many of us with a freely available alternative. Modern roof downspouts are usually plastic and it is not difficult to cut across one which is conveniently situated and place a large rainwater butt or tank under it, with an overflow back into the surface-water drain. This gives you a sizeable store for rainwater off the roof of your house which is topped up every time it rains without any further effort on your part. Such tanks are not expensive in terms of cost or resources.

Rainwater is useful in any garden or greenhouse; if you are modestly ingenious and the tank levels are right, you can run it through a hose. Rainwater does not contain substances such as chalk or lime which may be present naturally or will have been introduced into your main supply if it is naturally acidic. All public supplies are kept slightly alkaline to prevent corrosion in metal pipework, but as a result acid-loving plants like azaleas never flourish on tap-water.

Public water supplies are also slightly chlorinated to kill off any bacteria which may penetrate them. Chlorine is used for the same purpose, but in larger quantities, in swimming pools.

Chlorine is not beneficial to any living thing; and although the proportions in which it is used in drinking water probably do us no harm – or at least less harm than bacteria would – it may harm

63

plants which are watered over and over again in a greenhouse, plant pot or other restricted environment.

Rainwater has other uses and can be employed for everything from washing down surfaces to cleaning cars. Every drop saved and used spares resources required to provide the purified public supply.

Quality

The quality of the liquid wastes we discharge depends on the substances we add to water before it goes down the drain. For example, almost everyone uses detergents. Many liquid detergents still include phosphates (used as a water-softener) which cannot readily be extracted from sewage. Phosphates fertilise and encourage the spread of algae and other plants which clog watercourses and reduce water oxygen levels, killing fish and other water animals. They may eventually turn watercourses into foul and lifeless sewers.

Many detergents also include foaming agents to produce a lather. Lather produced in soapy water indicates that there is enough soap in the water to clean, but detergents do not work in the same way and do not need to show a lather at all. Foaming agents persist in water when it goes down the drain and cause foam to build up in watercourses.

Environmentally friendly detergents which do not include phosphates are now available commercially and we should buy them – as well as detergents free of foaming agents, if available. But ordinary washing soda used (in combination with soap for washing purposes) since Victorian times is a very good water-softener and general cleaning aid. If anything, it does good rather than harm after it leaves us in our waste water. Some of its many uses are outlined in the Appendix on pages 138–9.

Bleach (sodium hypochlorite) is potentially damaging, though many of us pour it down the drain without a thought. Bleach is a killer – indeed, its germ-killing quality is widely advertised – and again it is the chlorine in the bleach which does the killing. A good deal of that chlorine remains active and goes on killing after we have sent it down the drain.

If your foul water flows into a septic tank and is not mixed with anyone else's, you may have personal experience of what bleach can do. A septic tank only functions efficiently if anaerobic bacteria present in all sewage flourish and digest solid waste. If bleach goes down the drain regularly, it kills those bacteria. When that happens, the tank seizes up and requires regular and expensive pumping out.

Comparable results can follow the general large-scale emptying of bleach into public sewers. Much public sewage treatment also depends, or used to depend, on natural anaerobic fermentation. If the quantity of bacterial toxins in sewage makes that impossible, more expensive treatment is necessary.

Whatever other consequences there may be, all use of bleach adds to the quantities of chlorine loose in the environment. We need to remember that chlorine is potentially harmful to virtually every life form and in virtually every form in which it exists. Its commonest compound, common salt or sodium chloride, is least harmful; but no animal can take great quantities of salt, and very small quantities may wither most plants. Another sodium-chlorine compound – sodium chlorate – has long been used specifically as a weedkiller.

More modern manufactured chlorine compounds have become notorious. They include the persistent organo-chlorine pesticides like DDT (dichlor-diphenyl-trichloroethane); the PCBs (polychlorinated-biphenyls); and the compounds formed in the chemical reactions which lead to the forming of dioxins. Their devastating long-term effects are best known from the Seveso disaster in Italy, and the American use of the defoliant Agent Orange in Vietnam.

The chlorine in CFCs (chlorofluorocarbons), used as a coolant gas in refrigerating equipment, a propellant (now largely outlawed) in aerosols, and a foaming gas in plastic manufacture contributes both to the greenhouse effect and the destruction of the ozone layer (see pages 91–3). In its elemental form, chlorine was used as a poison gas in the First World War.

So we face a dilemma: bleach may be very useful at home, but we do no one (except perhaps its manufacturers) any good by using it when it can possibly be avoided. Apart from using tiny quantities to wipe off mildew stains there are not many domestic uses of bleach which can be commended. Most of its conventional uses result in its being flushed down the drain sooner or later.

What could we use instead? Germ-killing properties often figure in bleach sales promotion and it may be comforting to imagine loos and drains without bacteria. But we should not be too impressed by that propaganda. Few of us have close enough contact with our loos or drains in ways which might expose us to harmful bacteria. We are far more likely to encounter germs if we bathe in water polluted by sewage outfalls, among the bacteria which have survived all the bleach – as we have done for years.

On the other hand, bleach does clean loos. We have become attached to shiny, clean-looking toilet bowls, and detached from the lavatory brushes which were once used to keep them that way.

There are alternatives to bleach. There are toilet-cleaning substances on the market, labelled 'safe for septic tanks', which do not contain any significant quantity of bleach. For other purposes, washing soda may be used as a substitute. Soda is a simple, cheap, long-established alternative which can be used as an aid in a host of washing and cleaning operations. Mildly alkaline, it helps break down grease, and does no environmental harm after it has been used. Nor is soda harmful to us: bath salts are based on it. However, it is prudent to rinse it off the skin if used in concentrated solution.

If substances other than bleach may cause harm when you use them, the safest general rule is to assume that they will also cause harm if put down the drain. That applies to all forms of oil, all chemical solvents, and virtually all waste medicines. Cooking fat and grease are forms of oil which solidify on contact with cold surfaces and may block drains: pour them on your compost heap, burn them, or put them into an empty tin in your rubbish bag.

Solids which will not dissolve should also be burned, or wrapped and put out for refuse collection. They should not go down the drain. Nappy-liners, condoms, tampons, sanitary towels and similar detritus may block your own drains or cause blockage elsewhere. They hinder sewage treatment. If you visit a sewage works you will see for yourself the scale of the equipment and resources devoted to moving and shredding ('macerating' is the euphemism) insolubles which people have thoughtlessly flushed away. If you walk along a sea-shore near an untreated sea sewage outfall, the environmental impact of such items will be inescapable.

Only soluble organic wastes and cleaning substances declared safe on their packaging should go down the drain. If we all accepted that as an objective, subsequent problems in waste treatment and disposal would be significantly reduced. In particular, more sewage sludge might then be recycled back for use as fertiliser instead of being dumped on land or, worse, at sea.

General waste

In many respects we have become instinctively wasteful. We buy because merchandise is new or fashionable, even though we already have less fashionable equivalents which are still entirely serviceable. We buy gifts for our children, even when the chances are that those gifts will be put to one side almost as soon as they are opened; and that our children will continue to find pleasure in cherished existing possessions. We buy on impulses sparked by heavy advertising when a little more thought and research might lead us to an alternative which costs less, and is more serviceable. Product research before purchase is far less widespread than it should be, even though the Consumers' Association has for years published information about the comparative cost and performance of most products, and its publication *Which?*, along with associated publications, is available to non-subscribers in local libraries.

We all have habits which inspire waste and we are vulnerable to the advertising subtly and deliberately designed to exploit them. The environment suffers unnecessarily each time they are exploited. If we confined our purchases to articles which we really need, or at least to those whose value to us is commensurate with the cost and the resources used to produce them, that alone would contribute significantly to our welfare and that of the environment.

The pressure to accept wasteful giveaways is even more insidious than that in the advertising of the goods we buy. How many plastic carrier and other bags and packages do we accept without thought when we go shopping? How many of them might we re-use, over and over again, if we preserved them and remembered to take them with us next time round? How much junk mail do we accept without protest and without any effort to prevent its reaching us? One request by letter, post free, to Mailing Preference Service, Freepost 22, London W1E 7EZ is all it takes to have your name and address removed from all the main mailing lists in Britain.

All this unsolicited and unwanted rubbish costs resources; all of it represents waste; all of it has cost someone something. It is up to us to be less receptive.

Finally, there is pre-packaging. The philosophy of the throw-away package has eaten deeply into our way of life. Almost without thought, we reach for pre-packed items even when the same commodity is available unpacked. The unpacked item frequently costs less and, if perishable, is fresher.

The same health and quality regulations apply to perishable foods whether sold wrapped or loose. Food sold loose has to be fresh to comply with those regulations; food sold packed may comply only because sterilisation, preservatives and other additives have arrested decay. It is easy to understand why people who sell perishable foods prefer the easier handling and longer shelf life of pre-packed items. Whether our preference should always be the same merits some thought. The environment is suffering from excessive pre-packing.

5

The Way We Work

The vast majority of us work in a different place from the one in which we live. Most of us accept that pattern without a thought: that is the way it has always been.

Separate homes and workplaces wasted few resources as long as people worked in small groups and went on foot to join them. Even when industry began to need the combined effort of larger numbers of people, resource economy survived – albeit at the cost of crowding people close together in living conditions which were often well nigh intolerable.

The distances feasible between the places where people lived and worked began to grow when energy and resources were harnessed in ever greater quantities to provide artificial means of transport. The goods carried by canal transported the benefit of work done in one place to those working in another. Railways and road transport moved the people. The scene was set for urban sprawl, and for the environmental damage caused by using ever-increasing quantities of resources to bridge ever-increasing gaps between home and work. Over little more than a century constellations of villages, once isolated in open countryside, became locked deep within vast built-up conurbations. London's Hampstead is a typical example.

Economy of scale was the original, if undeclared and unperceived, logic of the trend which brought more and more people together from ever more distant homes. Large numbers could combine their efforts far more efficiently and productively by working together in the same place. Industrial projects and operations depended, as some still do, on many people being available for work at the same location. The old precept – united we stand, divided we fall – extends into ergonomics.

Up to a point, the resource and environmental advantages of combining the efforts and energies of large numbers of people in one place may outweigh, in real terms, the resource and environmental cost of bringing them together. A vast steelworks may consume far fewer resources, and be far better placed to detoxify its pollutants, than hundreds of widely scattered workshops which collectively produce the same volume of steel. Within limits, that resource and environmental profit is not be lost if people who work in the steelworks have to travel some distance to reach it.

But there are limits. If the distances travelled exceeded these limits, people working in such a steelworks would burn more resources, and cause more environmental damage by travelling to and from work, than the combination of their efforts would save when they arrived there.

It is excessively simplistic to say that if that happened, employers or employees would no longer be able to afford what either or both of them were doing. That would only be true if employers or employees had to bear all its cost. One way or another, they must cover the price actually paid for the resources used. But if it costs more to support a given standard of living earned in a congested area than it does in an area where people need not be so remote from their work, the difference measures part at least of the additional resource cost and shows part of what might be saved.

Note that it only shows part: the price paid for resources does not cover their replacement cost, or the damage caused to the general environment by using those resources. Those costs only appear in the environmental account.

Global figures leave no doubt that we are running the world environment at an accelerating loss. Virtually all the indicators are deteriorating. In how many local environments which are significantly affected by long-distance commuting is the position any better? We can judge that for ourselves.

Outright proof that losses on *local* environmental accounts have already overwhelmed the profit we think we are realising with our daily tidal flows between home and work may not emerge until that environment is bankrupt. But by then it will be too late to do anything about it. A prudent businessman accepts that if his accounts show accelerating losses and he does nothing, bankruptcy is inevitable. We should take the same view of the accelerating environmental losses caused by the way we work.

Thus far we have locked ourselves into a crazy dance. Wastefully, we duplicate the same facilities – homes with one set and workplaces with another. We then burn years of our time, energy and conscious lives, and with them resources to match, trafficking between the two. If no more than one out of every ten people in Britain spends two hours travelling to work each day the total of hours lost is equivalent to one and half million people on strike all the time. The resulting lifestyle is so stressful and unsatisfactory that most of us need to escape from it regularly into a third set of facilities somewhere else.

We have invested so many resources in this merry-go-round that we cannot now unscramble the hardware; and we have packed the hardware so tightly that every time we invest further resources to buy off further problems, we create new ones which demand still more investment. How can we or our environment ever profit if our way of life is such that we must drive new motorways and railways through houses, shops and factories; build new houses, shops and factories to accommodate the dispossessed; and then build new motorways and railways to reach them?

There is a solution. We are ingenious creatures and our ingenuity has already yielded instruments with which we could end this vicious circle. We possess automated and mechanised tools which obviate the need to assemble large numbers of people for physical labour. We have electronic information technology and telecommunication equipment with which we can co-ordinate managerial, administrative, clerical, intellectual and creative effort. There is no longer any practical reason why large numbers of people need to assemble in one place before significant work can be done.

Anyone who doubts this should reflect on the work he or she does, and on how much of it might be done from anywhere – by post, telephone (and shortly video-phone), radio, telex, fax, or computer with a modem link. Anyone who considers that these facilities make no difference should reflect on the proportion of his or her work which only arises because other

71

people are constantly flowing to and fro between home and work.

If we set out conscientiously to use the alternatives now to hand, we could eliminate half or more of the resource wastage and environmental damage caused by our present way of life without giving up anything – except, of course, the deeply ingrained and time-honoured habit of working somewhere well away from where we live. We would lose part of the social contact which work remote from home involves; but we would have far more time and opportunity for social contact where we live.

At first sight so radical a change in accustomed working practices may nevertheless suggest real sacrifice; but sooner or later economics are likely to force it on us anyway. Every country has to trade for something. Imagine how any country which has persisted in conventional and traditional ways of life might even begin to compete against the first to use modern technology systematically. How could it outbid a competitor who had shed both the resource cost and environmental damage of moving millions of people around every day? The advantages which await the first in the field are too substantial and too obvious for someone not to attempt to grasp them. The disadvantages should haunt us if we feel content to be latecomers.

There is already a small-scale trend towards such new working patterns in Europe, America and Japan; but at present Singapore is the front runner. Singapore has embarked upon applications of information technology so systematic that Singaporeans already number among the richest and least resource dependent on earth.

In terms of survival, we can do without the waste and environmental damage inherent in our present way of working; we can certainly do without the prospect of a future in which economics will do for us even if corruption of the environment has not got there first. One or other is virtually inevitable if we go on as we are.

You may think that you cannot personally do much towards the realisation of an information technology revolution. After all, none of us as individuals is in a position to lay down communication networks and infrastructures. However, many of those networks are already in place, and they are extending daily.

You might also think that the need to see the person you are dealing with is fundamental to human nature; that seeing people is occasionally essential to the smoothing of difficult paths; and that you will always have to attend meetings in order to do it. But fibre-optic telecommunication lines, being set up both nationally and internationally, will remove the restraint on visual communication previously imposed by the limitations of microwave radio transmission. Once fibre optics are in place all of us will be able to use video-phone equipment – which already exists – to see people as we talk to them. Visual confrontation will no longer depend on physical meetings.

Suppose that you are already convinced, but the organisation you work for is not? By their nature, organisations tend to resist change in the way they run their affairs. This is so even when they can see, as Britain can when it looks at Germany and Japan, that different forms of management produce better results with the same or fewer resources. But organisational conservatism is only a convenient alibi which allows life for the rest of us to drift on as it does. An employer may seem to have an inbred belief that you can only prove you are working for him satisfactorily by coming in through his door at 9.00 am every day and staying there until at least 5.00 pm; but if so, that belief only persists because you acquiesce in it.

The apparent conservatism of organisations mirrors a deeper truth: it is that they incline naturally to a quiet life. Left to their own devices they will only force the pace for change of their own volition if economics seriously threaten that quiet life. Only money, and particularly the lack of it, automatically pumps messages swiftly through institutional veins.

But quiet organisational lives also depend on our easy acceptance of the way things are. If we press for change, the desire for a quiet life may encourage organisations to envisage it. This is particularly so with changes such as the more effective use of information technology, which may enrich organisational life-blood rather than threaten it.

So the ball is still in our court. There is no rational excuse for us to sit back and say that 'they' must do something first. We have already reached the stage where what matters most is our willingness to install the appropriate equipment, to use it and

73

allow its use. In many cases, only our own attitudes stand in the way.

What would we get out of it ourselves? A reduction in wasteful mobility in the course of work would reduce our costs and our resource wastage as well as that of the organisations for which we work. Commuting eats into our time and energy as well as into that which we are able to offer employers when we reach them. Our saving could immediately be put to more productive personal use.

A reduction in travel time would effectively lengthen our lives. On average, we sleep eight hours a day and are conscious for 16 of them. Travel to work falls mostly in the conscious period. A commuter whose travel time averages three hours a day, five days a week, 47 weeks a year for the 45 years of a working life is wasting five and half years of the 70 which the Bible suggests is his natural span.

The environmental, resource and financial advantage of 'do it yourself' figures several times in this study and specifically in the next chapter. But arguing that 'do it yourself' should play a far larger part in our lives invites an almost standard reply: maybe it is beneficial and desirable, but I just don't have the time and energy.

New information technology-based working arrangements would release much of that time and energy. Work from or near home would make that time additionally valuable because it could be used flexibly and applied at choice across a wide range of tasks. We would no longer face the problem which so often confronts us: action we need to take, time available in which to take it, but action impossible because we are in the wrong place to pursue it.

Considerations such as these are already important. They will soon be even more important, with fewer young people coming on to the labour market; and with even more women entering the field of paid employment, both through necessity and through choice. If we remain wedded to traditional working patterns, living and working in different places increasingly far apart, choices between the demands of home and work will become ever more painful and family life may well disintegrate altogether under the pressure. If husbands and wives both work away from home, what happens when one is forced to move away because employment demands it, and the other must stay put for the same reason? If either decides that home comes first, what price his or her productive skills and abilities?

Although examples of extended families still survive in stable communities, the mobility which conventional industrial employment demands has long since honed most families down into units consisting at best of husband, wife and children. Lacking the support – and sometimes discipline – of an extended family, such units are more vulnerable; but larger units would not be sufficiently mobile for current employment patterns. Now the divisive pressures of mobility are reaching out to embrace husbands and wives separately. If those pressures are not relieved, we shall soon end up with a nation in which the large majority of households consist of single adults – with or without children in tow. That trend is already becoming apparent, and platitudes about the sanctity of the family do not diminish the pressures behind it.

Effective use of electronic information technology could save much of the environmental damage caused by resources frittered away during the daily round to work. It could save additional damage, social as well as material, by reducing divisive family pressures.

6

The Way We Play

Energy and the physical capacity for productive labour is a natural resource possessed by virtually all of us. Human energy is one of the most most readily adaptable and abundant renewable energy resources on earth. In relatively rich countries such as ours, this energy as used in our free time is one of the most wasted. More effective use of energy in our leisure time would benefit us individually; it would also unlock a range of substitutes for products whose manufacture and consumption is damaging to the environment.

We have to do something with our free time and energy if we are to remain physically and mentally fit; and for that we also need to be physically and mentally active in a number of different pursuits. Variety is very truthfully said to be the spice of life.

Until fairly recently, work implied hard physical labour for the vast majority of people. It followed naturally that, when people turned to diversity in their free time, that diversity focused on opportunities for rest and relaxation. 'All work and no play makes Jack a dull boy' embodies a truth which was then altogether valid.

It remains valid now in the limited sense that hardly anyone benefits from toiling away at the same thing all the time. But we deceive ourselves if we interpret it as meaning that after work, which is no longer hard work, we should still seek play which is soft.

Modern inventions and discoveries, the technologies which have flowed from them and the resources they consume have combined to eliminate hard physical labour from most work, as work is conventionally understood. This applies as much in the home as in every other workplace. All work is tiring;

but nowadays in industrialised countries very little work is physically exhausting.

Modern technology and resources have also speeded up the time it takes to do the work, giving us all more free time. Used fully and effectively, along the lines explored in the last chapter, they could yield even more.

Modern medicine and health care have significantly improved the chances of our being fit to benefit from that time. But 'play' in the traditional sense now threatens those chances. With hard daily physical labour removed from work, our welfare now requires a diversification into hard physical daily labour in our free time.

This need for hard physical activity away from work is widely recognised; but the instinct that it should nevertheless equate with play and should not be productive lives on. As a result, the high price paid by the environment for the removal of physical labour from work is being raised still higher by the resources we consume and the waste we generate in play.

The environment would benefit singificantly if we applied spare-time energies to productive activities, or, at the very least, to activities which are less destructive. Many of these activities would be at least as beneficial to our health and state of mind as conventional leisure pursuits. Most would put pluses into our personal budget and quality of life as well as into the environment. It is worth examining a few of these productive activities.

Gardening

Most of us have gardens, whether large or small. Others have places where they can grow something. The children at Lamplugh school in Cumbria, for example, produce organic food on part of their school playing field, and have won an environmental award for their effort.

The extent to which gardening alone might supply our necessary daily ration of exercise depends on the size of the garden and on how productive we intend to make it. But every garden offers the opportunity to use time and energy productively.

The produce of your own garden brings benefits in the form of the exercise involved; the fresh uncontaminated food on your table; and the saving, however modest, of the retail price of that food. It benefits the environment by reducing your demand for the resource- and energy-dependent produce of others.

You should not underestimate your garden's potential. It has long been recognised that, area for area, higher yields can be obtained from an ordinary domestic vegetable garden than from any other form of agriculture. Part of the advantage comes from the scale of the operation. When you are cultivating mainly by hand, you can grow your crops more closely together than any farmer who has to run machines over them. This allows more yield from less land; it also serves to control weeds: once crops are established they crowd weeds out.

You are not cheating if you have a larger garden and use a machine sparingly to help you to make the most of it. You should normally have most of your land cultivated and ready for planting early on in the year. Meeting that deadline by attempting to dig by hand may, over a short period, demand far more than the daily ration of labour which is either necessary or desirable. It may also fail in its purpose, for by the time you reach the end of digging a large patch, weeds may be thriving again at the beginning.

If, on the other hand, you use a suitable rotovator – whether you own it or hire one for the purpose – you will still be getting plenty of exercise hauling it around, and you will also be able to cultivate your land in a very short time. In larger-scale gardens this is likely to be economical in cost, resource and environmental terms.

Other advantages flow from the relatively small scale of gardens, and from the fact that you can apply labour – your own – far more intensively than is possible in agriculture. You can expect to make sufficient compost from your own wastes for them to play a significant part in maintaining soil quality and fertility. Small quantities of animal manures, if available, are additionally useful.

Many reasons have combined to force modern agriculture worldwide to rely on manufactured inorganic fertilisers, rather than organic substances. One of the most potent is the sheer impossibility of making, moving and spreading, over vast areas of land, the mountains of organic alternatives which would be needed if that land were to yield as much as your garden. Consider manuring the corn belt across the North American prairies, for example.

Traditional small mixed arable and livestock farms attacked the fertiliser problem by rotating the use of their land. Part lay fallow while cattle grazed it, manuring it without human intervention as they did so, and other land was rested when the fallow land was ploughed. After ploughing, different arable crops were grown in succeeding years to utlise different nutrients before the land was again rested. The cycle often included legumes – typically field or broad beans which were fed to the farm's working horses – which add nitrogen to the soil.

Modern organic farmers are reverting to that type of land management. Improved seed strains and the continued use of machines for cultivation result in far higher yields than those attained by our ancestors. Nevertheless, the volume yielded is usually still inferior to that achieved by mechanised inorganic farming, if only because disease and pest losses are greater when no chemicals are used. This is one reason why organic food costs more.

Using all the compost you can make, you may still find that you cannot introduce enough nutrient into your garden to yield reasonable crops, particularly if you cannot supplement it with generous quantities of animal manure. Your results will not be satisfactory if your soil does not contain enough nitrogen, phosphorous or potash, or if it is too acidic to allow the plants to take up whatever nutrients are there, whatever the source of those substances.

However, if some, or all, of your plants look like pale imitations of the pictures in catalogues or on seed packets, you do not now need to rely on ancient diagnostic knowledge or guesswork. Most garden centres sell cheap soil-test kits; with these you can soon discover if your soil is deficient in any of the chemical elements which your plants need, and whether you need to feed in any more than is naturally there.

If your soil is too acid, calcium carbonate – in lime, chalk, marl or slag – will solve the problem. Though mineralised, these arguably have an organic ancestry in the shells of the marine animals of which they are a fossilised remainder. If it lacks nitrogen, phosphorous or potash, gardening books provide lists of organic sources. Organic fertilisers are relatively costly.

Even if you have to resort to inorganic fertilisers, you can achieve good results with quantities far smaller than those used in agriculture. You need only sprinkle a few granules in the immediate locality of the plants you are growing, whereas farm machines blanket or spray whole fields.

If you have to use inorganic fertilisers, you will find it cheaper to buy a farm-sized sack of one which is evenly balanced from an agricultural merchant – a personal and environmental economy. A sack will meet the needs of even a large garden for several years as long as you keep its contents dry. Garden centres also sell inorganic fertilisers but usually in smaller and more expensive quantities owing to extra packaging and handling costs.

All agricultural fertiliser sacks have the numerical unit quantity and proportion of the essential constituents printed on them. For example, 20:20:20 means those numbers of units of nitrogen, phosphorous and potash – always in that sequence. Merchants who sell such fertilisers will usually advise which is best for general use if you are in doubt.

The advantages of producing food in your own garden are not confined to exercise or to achieving environmentally less damaging cultivation and fertility. You can pick and consume all you grow. Your produce does not have to meet the mathematically exacting standards of supermarket buyers who reject fruit or vegetables if colour, shape or size does not fit the marketing image or the tidy symmetry of the pack. This alone now contributes to inordinate waste as farmers grade out and dump thousands of tonnes of good food which fails buyer specifications. For all the diligence of plant breeders, peas do not naturally all stay small.

You can also avoid waste because you can crop your food as it is needed for immediate consumption or freezing and take it fresh to the kitchen. In this way there is no loss in food value. As soon as fruit and cut vegetables are harvested, destructive enzymes naturally present begin to decay their nutritional value. Plant breeders have worked hard and successfully to provide commercial varieties with strains which do not show obvious signs of decay in the time which elapses between crops leaving the grower and arriving on the shop shelf. But their achievement conceals natural processes and does not arrest them. As much as half the nutritional value of fresh food can be lost in transit.

Finally, you can grow those varieties which have the best flavour. Seldom do these grade or travel well, and they no longer appear in shops as a result. (Compare the strawberries available commercially with the old Royal Sovereign strawberry if you know it and doubt either point.)

Whatever you produce, and thus need not buy, saves the environment something; and that is so even if you only have a window box. Part of that saving comes in the production process, and a significant part in subsequent transport and handling. Commodities such as potatoes, for example, arrive in shops in the same form as they leave the producer, but then cost three or more times the amount the producer is paid for them. A material part of the difference reflects intervening handling and environmental costs.

If you grow consumable food, you contribute more directly to savings – environmental and your own – than if you concentrate on the aesthetic attraction of flowers. You could survive without flowers, but you have to have food. Having said this, you will find that there is usually somewhere in most gardens where flowers will grow and food will not. Food is a sensible priority for your time and labour; flowers, particularly perennials, may demand little of either.

Grass and lawns are a different matter altogether. Convention encourages all of us to try and translate images conjured by the great rolling lawns of stately homes into our own gardens, even on the pocket handkerchief scale. Convention and taste intermingle and no one should lecture on taste. From the environmental point of view, however, lawns are a disaster and the more care we lavish on them the greater that disaster is. On the grotesque scale it is said that more fertiliser is used on the lawns in the parks and cemeteries of the United States than is available for food production in the whole sub-continent of India.

Fashion, and sometimes snobbery, are a powerful influence

behind this waste in our gardens. Some time ago, a company promoting pensions illustrated the point. They advertised their product against a picture of an elderly couple tending a small rose bed set in a large lawn behind a mock-Tudor mansion. 'Will he have to give up his golf club subscription?' ran the legend; 'Will she have to dig up her roses and plant vegetables?' The obvious message was that we should dash out and buy the pension advertised so that we might stave off these unmitigated disasters.

The reality is mundane, but it is a reality. The odds are that the couple in the advertisement would eat better and be fitter, richer and probably happier if they devoted their land and time to the production of food – regardless of whether they needed to. It is a certainty that the environment would benefit if they did.

Keeping productive animals

Animals can complement small-scale garden food production just as they do large-scale agriculture. Apart from any food produced, if they eat kitchen or garden waste they will help recycle it into valuable manure. As well as the honey they supply, bees in a garden beehive will increase the yield of any fruit or vegetable which must be pollinated before it will fruit.

You have to have enough space in which to keep animals, and you will usually need to enclose them. Even poultry will damage your produce and that of your neighbours if ranging free, and birds are also a prey to dogs or foxes. Because animals do not necessarily distinguish between edible and non-edible plants within their reach, you may have to fence them away from poisonous vegetation, such as laburnum, as well as from plants you are cultivating.

You need very little space to keep a few hens. One coop designed commercially for six hens has a ground plan of 97.5 cm by 105 cm (3'3" x 3'6"), stands 91 cm (3') tall and has two internal levels – the upper for roosting and laying and the lower for scratching. Small and ornamentally attractive chickens such as bantams and silkies can manage with little more than half that space. A narrow cage built along a garden wall, as is the case with many aviaries, will suffice. If you keep poultry in small numbers, your ordinary kitchen wastes will supply much of the food they need. However, most animals need some purchased supplementary feed if they are to do well, and animals which cannot forage for themselves over open ground almost always do. The larger the animal or number of animals kept, the larger the space, containment and quantity of supplementary feed you will require.

Your poultry will supply you with eggs. If you keep milking goats they will supply you with milk. As long as you and your family do not get too attached to them, poultry, rabbits, sheep or the offspring of goats may also supply meat. They all yield meat of fine eating quality. But if you keep any animal for meat, you have to be prepared to face the not-necessarily tasteful period between the animal being an animal and its becoming a joint of meat; buying from a butcher spares us from having to think too closely about that transition.

Bees apart, every animal which is kept domestically will need daily feeding and care. Any lactating animal, such as a goat or cow, needs milking once and usually twice a day. Keeping productive animals is a rewarding pastime, even if you eventually eat them; and animal husbandry is usually a profitable use of the time, energy and other resources which it consumes. But animals do tie you down; and although friends or neighbours may be willing to ensure that poultry feed hoppers and water containers are topped up when you are away, you may search in vain for someone willing to milk a goat or a cow, or care for a large animal. Any decision to keep a large animal first requires the certain knowledge that there will always be someone willing and able to look after it.

Revising household systems

Whatever our dedication to conservation, there is a limit to the number of separate routines any of us can hope to adopt in order to save resources – or remember to follow systematically. New living habits help once they are established, but old habits die hard. It pays, therefore, to have a new look at everything round the house and where possible to set up or install systems which make automatic savings once they are established.

Specific examples have already been given in previous chapters. Low-consumption light bulbs fitted to the outlets most commonly used save energy, especially, if you also routinely switch off unnecessary lights; insulation automatically saves heat; sealed water-filled plastic bottles placed in toilet cisterns save drinking water; water butts retain rainwater to be used for other purposes. The most dependable resource-saving measures are those which require no further thought once they are adopted; and those which we can adopt by our own efforts. Everything we do for ourselves saves the resources used by someone who would otherwise be coming to do it for us.

Of course, few of us are strangers to the financial advantages of using our own time and energy. If we were, do-it-yourself materials would not be sold on the scale and in the diversity in which they are. But DIY has environmental advantages, regardless of cost considerations.

Saving and re-using materials

If contractors have to clear the decks before they replace or renew something in our homes, the chances are that what they have to remove first will end up in the builder's skip for dumping. Contractors may lack the patience needed to save materials which we could re-use, even if the cost of the effort made this worthwhile. If we use our own labour to clear the path, we may save ourselves cost; if we save re-usable materials, the environment also benefits.

Purchase planning

At the risk of repetition, it should be stressed that everything we buy involves a further assault, however minor, on the environment – and that applies equally, whether the purchase replaces something which we already have or supplies something which we did not have previously. Yet the statement needs repeating. Constant buying has become almost instinctive to our way of life and vast efforts, and resources, are devoted to keeping it that way. Even our increasing anxieties about the environment are being perverted to the cause. We are urged to buy goods because they are green, or environmentally friendly, and commercial interests are sponsoring all sorts of gimmicks with an environmental slant to them. Hardly anyone bothers to mention that buying anything at all implies environmental damage.

We need to keep a clear mind: the sole purpose of any effort to make us buy is to make someone else richer. We may incidentally benefit from a purchase, but if we make it, the environment and its resources are a casualty. If the environment enters into the picture at all, it is often only on the basis that if we buy product A the environment will suffer less than if we buy product B, and even that is not guaranteed. Our use of product A may be less harmful – aerosols free of ozone-destroying gases are an example. But the energy and materials used to make the throwaway aerosol still involve the same environmental damage, whether the gas inside is harmful or benign. A refillable and re-usable pumped aerosol involves less damage – but it still involves damage.

Our environment does not have marketing managers or advertising agents of its own. Company marketing managers are concerned about it and advertising agents are conscious of it only because they know we are worried. This again illustrates the fact that if we do not act to save the environment ourselves, no one else will.

So, any environmentally constructive use of our free time and energy should also include a conscious counter-blast to the pressures of sales promoters. When it comes to buying, we need to ask ourselves these basic questions: Do we need it? Can we make efficient use of it? Will it save or use more resources if we have it? Will it last, or will it soon require a replacement?

The answer to the first two questions depends very much on our personal circumstances and on the way any particular article relates to them. If a power tool or other piece of equipment makes it possible for you to do a job which would otherwise have to be done for you at a greater cost in resources, it makes sense to buy it. But if the only real attraction is that someone you know has one, or that some advertiser has suggested that you will be behind the times without it, buying it is unlikely to make any sense at all. If we must keep up with the Joneses, let it at least be with the Joneses who rate function and utility first and mere possession nowhere.

The second two questions involve the lasting and technical qualities of the goods we buy. Most of us need help on this, but the help is there. We can compare the energy and other resources used by different appliances merely by looking at the instruction manuals which accompany them in showrooms. Local authority building departments can usually quote chapter and verse on the advantages and disadvantages of building materials, and on how they comply with building regulations. Trading standards' officers may advise. The British Standards Association lays down quality standards for a vast range of products and those which comply with them are so marked. Most consumer goods carry labels with details of their contents and uses. Most dealers and manufacturers will supply full technical information about their products. Finally, general publications frequently review specific goods, and publications such as the Consumer Associations' periodical *Which* compare and evaluate the cost and performance of competing brands.

We seldom lack the necessary information, even if it is sometimes difficult to understand some of it. All too often, however, we fail to seek it out and use it: only if all else fails do we read the instructions. Very few of us are innocent in this respect. Yet just a small part of our time and energy applied to research would put our environment just a little less at risk.

Admittedly, consumer concern and detailed analyses such as those published in *Which*? have increasingly highlighted manufactured goods with built-in obsolescence. It is no longer the case, as it used to be, that something made to last almost always costs more than something which is not. Many manufacturers now ensure that all their products work and continue to work for very long periods; the Japanese in particular have forced the pace. But we are still a long way away from being able to dispense with our own research.

That research is vitally important. The longer our goods last and continue to function, the shorter our demand on resources and the damage which their processing and manufacture causes the environment.

Unproductive time

Few of us are likely to make all our time productive, and it is not desirable for us to try. Even then, we have choices between activities which are more or less destructive. If we walk or cycle for enjoyment, the environment is better off than if we take the car. If we travel further afield, the environment suffers less if we go by coach or train than if we go by car. If we travel still further afield, ships are kinder to the environment than aircraft.

The environment benefits if we take holidays nearer home rather than further away. We may benefit too: fewer fruitless hours spent lingering in overcrowded transit lounges; a choice of more beaches washed by ocean tides, and fewer by the effluent outfalls of hastily constructed tourist complexes on the shores of enclosed seas and waterways. And if the greenhouse effect unrolls as seems likely (see Chapter 7, page 103) we may anyway soon be able to rely on better summer weather nearer home than in the more traditional distant resorts. The weather is on the move. Places which previously offered attractive conditions may no longer enjoy them, and vice versa.

We also have options as regards general entertainment. Television, radio, video and sound-reproducing equipment deliver entertainment to us at home. That entertainment is often of higher quality than is now attainable in live performance – quite simply because more time and cash is usually available for its production; the best, or the best parts, of several performances can be chosen; and we can see or hear more of the final result into the bargain. The environmental cost of entertainment brought to us electronically at home is vastly less than that of transporting us to places of performance.

Nevertheless devotees still argue that live performances are more exciting. Yet if excitement is what it is all about, do we have to hammer the environment yet again by travelling to find it? Are we incapable of satisfying our need for excitement nearer home?

7

The Greenhouse and Ozone Effects – and Surviving Them

When measured from space, the earth radiates energy at levels which would be characteristic of a planet whose temperature was minus 18 degrees Celsius. If the earth had that temperature it would be permanently frozen. In fact, the average surface temperature is higher by some 33 degrees. The difference is due to the proportion of incoming energy from the sun trapped by the world's ocean and land masses and retained by the greenhouse effect of its atmosphere.

Over the last 100 years, average world surface temperatures have increased by half a degree Celsius. Half a degree does not sound very much even when translated into a 1.5 per cent increase in the insulating efficiency of the atmosphere. But the amount of energy needed to raise world temperature deliberately by half a degree would, by a very rough calculation, be around 300 times the total amount of heat produced every year from the billions of tonnes of fossil and other fuels which we burn worldwide.

The increase in temperature over the last 100 years has more or less paralleled the rise in the proportion of heat-retaining greenhouse gases such as carbon dioxide and methane in the atmosphere. That proportion has been increased by the waste gases of the fuel we burn and by other activities for which we are responsible, considered in greater detail later in this chapter.

Ice cores have been drilled out of the Antarctic ice-cap, which date back more than 160,000 years to before the onset of the last ice age. Analysis of the gases locked in these cores has revealed that rises and falls in world temperature have always matched rises and falls in the proportion of greenhouse gases in the atmosphere. It has not yet been possible to prove whether these greenhouse gas fluctuations have been the cause of the cycle of ice ages and inter-glacial periods which has occured over the last million and a half years. They may merely have amplified the consequence of changes initiated by other forces. But the main body of world scientific opinion is now satisfied that the temperature increase of our own time is caused by the increase in the proportion of atmospheric greenhouse gases, for which man is responsible; and that the rise in temperature is accelerating as that proportion continues to increase. The decade from 1980 to 1989 has been the warmest on record and the years 1988, 1987 and 1981 – in that order – have so far been the three warmest on record.

The global environmental effect of the gases we are venting into the atmosphere is not measured only in temperature increases. Man-made gases, particularly but not solely the CFCs (chlorofluorocarbons), are migrating into the upper atmosphere. There, they are eroding the tenuous layer of ozone which shields all life on earth, our own include, against damage from intense ultra-violet light from the sun. (This issue is also considered in more detail later in this chapter.)

When high-level ozone was first measured in Antarctica in 1956, the ozone shield was intact. In 1982 it was discovered that a hole had appeared in it, shaped a little like a three-dimensional pancake. That hole has grown larger yearly ever since. At its extreme it now covers an area the size of the continental United States and is five miles deep.

The influences of atmospheric circulation and the earth's magnetic field are such that any significant depletion of high-level ozone would produce outright holes in the ozone layer, starting with the high Antarctic and Arctic latitudes, where they have already been observed. But as is often the case with fabrics, the emergence of holes is accompanied by a thinning of the fabric everywhere. Worldwide ground-level measurements reveal steady increases in the amount of ultra-violet radiation reaching the surface, and high-level investigation shows a steady depletion of ozone.

It is these events which have turned pollution and environmental damage into issues which concern everyone. They involve the air we breathe, the climate we experience, and the radiation which reaches us from outer space. They are indivisible; we are all in the firing line if something goes wrong.

It is hardly surprising that the message is striking home. In a recent survey, damage to the ozone layer ranked first, and the greenhouse effect sixth, in people's environmental anxieties, with other concerns all relating to them. Nearly 87 per cent of those questioned were anxious about the ozone layer, and 80 per cent about the greenhouse effect.

Yet these worries are merely a part of the picture. The lifeless lakes, rivers and inland seas, and the pollution death which is creeping out over the the Baltic, North Sea and Mediterranean, are another part. So too are the combustion gases which mix with water vapour in the atmosphere and destroy forests and water life with acid rain, in addition to those forests which are burned. Localised damage may only seem to touch those who visit or live close to the places where it is suffered. But that damage feeds straight back into the global atmospheric picture. Land and sea-based plant life absorbs carbon dioxide and produces oxygen. The world's natural recovery system is also being destroyed.

We can all do something – and collectively we can do a great deal – to limit further damage and risk to these fundamental life-support systems, and this study makes a number of suggestions. But much damage has already been done, and we and our children and their children will have to live with the results, even if all the damage stops tomorrow – which it will not.

There is a case for reviewing the nature of the damage and its likely consequences if only to emphasise the importance of any step we take to minimise it.

The nature of the damage

First, by increasing the proportion of gases which retain in-coming solar heat beyond those levels naturally existing in the lower atmosphere, we are raising average world temperatures. The extra energy is increasing the power of world weather systems and altering the behaviour of the climate; it is expanding the volume of existing ocean water and rapidly adding to that volume by accelerating the melting of land-based ice fields. Low-lying land on which many people live and upon which many more rely for their food is at risk of flooding, and significant sudden increases in sea levels could occur.

Climatic change threatens production from the world's main existing food-growing areas. It may perhaps be possible to grow food elsewere in the higher latitudes of the northern hemisphere which have have been too cold hitherto; but the speed of the changes for which we are responsible is like lightning when compared with that of previous natural events. We may not be able to move the essential infrastructures of food production swiftly enough to keep pace with them; and natural life may be unable to adapt quickly enough to follow them.

Second, the greenhouse gases for which we are responsible include compounds which break down when exposed to ultra-violet radiation, and release elements which are exceptionally greedy for oxygen. Paradoxically, perhaps, this is increasing the proportion of ozone – itself a significant greenhouse gas – in the lower atmosphere, but decreasing the proportion in the tenuous upper atmosphere as man-made compounds migrate upwards.

Essentially, the processes involved are as follows: the vast proportion of the oxygen in the lower atmosphere is in the form on which our life depends – a molecule in which two atoms of oxygen are bonded together. When that oxygen migrates upwards and is exposed to intense ultra-violet radiation in the upper atmosphere, the bond between the two atoms is broken and the atoms reform into ozone – a molecule in which three oxygen atoms are combined. The ozone in turn breaks down and the process is repeated. Ultra-violet energy is absorbed by each reaction and the amount of ultra-violet radiation which continues on down to the earth's surface is thus diminished.

When other gaseous compounds migrate into the upper atmosphere, they also are broken down into their elemental components and may then recombine. Compounds which include oxygen, such as the nitrogen oxides, may interfere with the

91

ozone process by collecting more oxygen when they reform than they release when they break down: an example is nitrogen oxide reforming into nitrogen dioxide. But compounds which carry no oxygen with them, and particularly those whose elements are chemically very active, rebond tightly with oxygen and by so doing consume the resources available for the vital ozone process altogether. Chlorine and fluorine are both extremely reactive elements and both are present in the notorious CFCs (the chlorofluorcarbons). The CFCs survive unchanged for very long periods in the lower atmosphere and are now acknowledged to be the main cause of ozone depletion as they migrate to high levels.

That part of the ultra-violet radiation which passes through the upper atmosphere then causes reactions in the compounds it encounters at ground level – typically, the nitrogen oxides emitted by motor vehicle exhausts and general fossil fuel combustion. These reactions result in the release of single oxygen atoms, which combine with molecular two-atom oxygen to produce low-level ozone. Ozone is poisonous to us and most life forms in very small quantities, which is why the low level reaction is also a recognised health hazard.

Through these processes, atmospheric pollution attacks several vital life-support systems simultaneously. The ozone shield limits the amount of incoming solar ultra violet radiation which reaches the surface of the earth and without it all life on earth would be destroyed. Even thinning of the shield has serious consequences. Ultra-violet light damages animal and plant cells and, in our own case, leads to cataracts and skin cancers; the greater the level of ultra-violet light reaching the earth's surface, the greater is the incidence of this damage. Ultra-violet light also reacts at surface level with pollutants producing higher ozone levels there. Ozone is poisonous to animal and plant life in very small quantities, apart from being a greenhouse gas.

The increasing risk is measured by research. Apart from the ozone holes over Antarctica, investigators have reported a 3 per cent thinning in the ozone layer over the United States and Europe between 1969 and 1986; and measurements of incoming ultra-violet radiation taken at ground level in

Switzerland show an annual 1 per cent increase between 1980 and 1990.

The pollutants which do the damage

The man-made gaseous compounds which are damaging the environment as we pump them into the atmosphere are present only in minute proportions – parts per million (ppm) – but that does not prevent them having profound effects. Several are far more significant for the harm they cause or the rate at which their proportion is growing, than their vestigial quantity suggests.

At 350 ppm, for example, carbon dioxide (CO_2) is far and away the most substantial of the polluting gases, while at 0.0006 ppm, the CFCs are the most tenuous. But CFC levels are rising at 6 per cent a year, while those of CO_2 are only increasing at 0.4 per cent a year; and CFCs retain 10,000 times the heat of CO_2 in the lower atmosphere, as well as being the most vicious of the ozone absorbers above it.

The greenhouse effect of the five gases or compounds which are mainly responsible is therefore best illustrated by multiplying the proportion in which they are actually present by the extent to which their effect exceeds that of CO_2:

Gas	Actual concentration (ppm)	Effect relative to CO_2	CO_2 equivalent (ppm)	Annual % increase
CO_2	350.0	× 1	350	0.4
Methane	1.7	× 30	51	1.1
Nitrous oxides	0.3	× 150	45	0.3
Low-level ozone	0.001	× 2000	2	0.25
CFCs	0.0006	× 10,000	6	6.0

What are the sources of these gases?

93

Carbon dioxide

Every animal breathes out carbon dioxide produced by the biological combustion of the energy in its food. CO_2 also results from the burning or natural decay of all fossil fuel or other organic material and from volcanic and other natural eruptions from the earth. The output from all these sources, except the last, is increasing.

Levels of atmospheric CO_2 are regulated naturally. Some dissolves in water and becomes earthbound, sometimes in acid rain. More importantly, all plant life absorbs CO_2 during daylight hours. Using solar energy to power the natural process of photosynthesis, it locks the carbon component of CO_2 into its substance as part of its food, and frees the oxygen component back into the air. Our atmosphere would probably not include free oxygen if plants had not been doing this since the dawn of life. Animals which breathe air, ourselves included, could not have evolved, and would not survive, without it.

The fossil fuels – coal, oil and natural gas – which we are burning are the remains of life-forms which contributed to this refinement of the world's atmosphere. It took something like 400 million years, and 400 million years of sunshine, before they mopped up and locked out of the environment the carbon (and sulphur) oxides and hydrogen compounds which we now use as fuel and chemical feedstock. The sobering scale of what we have already done and are continuing to do is measured by the fact that we look set to undo that 400 million-year achievement within 400 years.

We have already far exceeded the earth's natural capacity to keep CO_2 in balance. Were it otherwise, atmospheric levels would not be rising and scientists would not be seeking an immediate (and apparently politically impossible) 60 per cent reduction in emissions worldwide. However, we are also making the position worse by eroding the natural regulator.

The obvious and deliberate human devastation of tropical and other forests, which is part of that erosion, evokes widespread anxiety. But trillions of minute surface phytoplankton, along with other ocean vegetation, are almost certainly more crucial to the CO_2 balance. After all, the oceans cover four-fifths of the earth's surface. These unseen components of the regulator are already at risk from water pollution, increasing sea temperatures, and rising levels of ultra-violet radiation.

Methane

When air is present, bacteria, fungi or other natural agents decay animal or vegetable organic matter and CO_2 is released. When air is excluded, anaerobic bacteria do the consuming and methane (around 70 per cent) and CO_2 (around 30 per cent) are released. Much of the natural gas percolating out of the earth which we burn is a fossil relic of this process; sewage, refuse tips, swamps, rice paddies, and herbivorous animals such as cattle are living methane sources.

Unlike CO_2 and CFCs, methane does not survive for long periods once it is loose in the atmosphere; its carbon and hydrogen components break down and separate. The environmental risk of methane is its supercharged heat-retaining capacity and the ever-increasing rate at which human activity is causing its release.

A relatively recent period of prehistory illustrates how this may affect us. Over the comparatively short period between 6000 and 3000 BC, average world temperatures rose to levels as much as 3 degrees Celsius above those to which we are accustomed. Until recent times, this was the warmest period to follow the last ice age and for that reason it is dubbed the 'climatic optimum'.

A short-lived surge in the level of atmospheric greenhouse gases is the most probable cause of the climatic optimum, and methane is the most likely culprit. Had CO_2 been the cause, the effect would probably have lasted far longer than 3000 years since CO_2 survives far longer in the atmosphere than methane. Moreover, the receding ice age would have released methane in vast amounts as ice-age tundra and permafrost melted into swamp right across the northern hemisphere.

This scenario adds to the urgency of reducing the emission of the greenhouse gases which we *can* control. If the actions for which we are directly responsible produce temperatures sufficient to thaw the remaining permafrost across North America, northern Europe and Siberia, the surge of methane (and CO_2) then released may boost the consequences of our actions beyond all predictable limits.

Nitrous oxides

Seventy-eight per cent of the air we breathe is nitrogen. Oxides of nitrogen are produced when anything is burned in air. Power stations, aircraft and motor vehicles all emit large quantities. Nitrogen compounds are also a key component of agricultural fertilisers, and nitrous oxides are released as they degenerate in the soil.

Nitrous oxides contribute significantly to the greenhouse effect, retaining, part for part, 150 times the heat of CO_2. They are involved in the processes which produce ground-level ozone and in those which destroy ozone in the upper atmosphere. It has been estimated that nitrous oxides were responsible for as much as 70 per cent of the oxygen–ozone loss which occurred naturally before we threw additional spanners into the works. At the natural level, however, the balance of reactions left sufficient ozone.

Ground-level ozone

Ozone is produced when electricity sparks across an air gap. It is then perceptible as a tenuous, pale blue smoke which has a pungent odour. However, the ground-level ozone which has environmental significance is the product of the reaction between ultra-violet radiation and man-made atmospheric pollution, which has already been described.

Ozone is a potent greenhouse gas, even in the proportions in which it is generally present in the atmosphere. General levels can multiply 100 times or more in hot, still, sunny weather in places with high levels of atmospheric pollution – particularly motor vehicle pollution. At such levels, it is also toxic and at the very least damaging to health. Ozone at and above toxic levels has been recorded in Los Angeles, London and other city centres.

Chlorofluorocarbons

The CFCs – compounds of chlorine, fluorine and carbon – are gases deliberately invented for use as heat-exchange gases in freezers and refrigerators. They have also been used as foaming agents in the manufacture of many foam plastics, and, until recently, as propellant gases in aerosols. They are very stable, do not ignite or explode and in ordinary conditions do not degenerate for very long periods. They are likely to remain active in the atmosphere for 50 years or more after all release ceases.

The considerable industrial utility of CFCs is matched by their disproportionately damaging environmental effect. CFCs are 10,000 times more heat retentive than CO_2 in the lower atmosphere, and when they break down under the intense ultra-violet radiation of the upper atmosphere, their constituents react with those of the vital oxygen–ozone process and immobilises it.

This hazard was first recognised in the early 1970s when studies were undertaken to evaluate the possible impact on the ozone layer of high-flying aircraft and the American space shuttle, and CFCs are now acknowledged as the number one threat to the ozone layer. They are not the only one, but others such as nitrogen oxides play a far smaller part.

By international agreement (the Montreal Protocol), production and use of CFCs is to be phased out by the year 2000, but in the meantime there will be a 30 per cent increase in production. Steps are being taken to reduce the release of CFCs (the ozone-friendly aerosol is an obvious first fruit of this exercise) but continued release is inevitable on the basis of present international agreements, which are still regarded as inadequate by many experts in the field.

The United Nations agency concerned with ozone depletion* has stated that each 1 per cent decrease in ozone-layer protection will lead to a 3 per cent increase in non-melanoma cancers and to an extra 100,000 additional people being blinded by cataracts each year. Since 1967, the ozone decrease has averaged around

*The United Nations Environment Programme's International Committee on the Effects of Ozone Depletion.

1 per cent every two years over the middle latitudes of Europe and North America.

As far as the greenhouse effect is concerned, it is estimated that even if everyone abides by the Montreal Protocol, CFCs will contribute to about 18 per cent of the total global warming we can expect. Those ozone-friendly CFC substitutes invented so far retain almost as much heat – ICI's HFC 134a substitute is said to be 4130 times more potent than CO_2.

This is the background against which we are all urged to ensure that when old freezers and refrigerators are scrapped, the CFCs which they contain are safely evacuated and are not released.

Living with ozone and the consequences of ozone depletion

The ozone layer never stopped all incoming ultra-violet radiation. Had it had done so no one would ever have got a tan from sunbathing, for it is the ultra-violet light which is responsible. Moreover, some ultra-violet light may be beneficial since its action on the skin is a source of Vitamin D.

Nowadays we usually obtain all the Vitamin D we need by eating oily fish, eggs or dairy products; but the chances are that such food sources were often not available to many of our remote ancestors. For them, the ultra-violet skin reaction may sometimes have been vital to survival. Vitamin D may provide the answer to why some races evolved with pale skins. People with light skins which admit more ultra-violet light may have been the only survivors in high latitudes where the sun is weaker.

There is, therefore, nothing new in the presence of ultra-violet radiation. Nor is there anything new in its dangers. On the minus side, it has always been capable of causing cellular injury – cataracts, skin damage and skin cancer – and has always caused it. What we have to understand is that the balance of advantages and disadvantages is changing very rapidly. More ultra-violet light is coming through; we either expose ourselves less to sunlight than previously or we increase our chances of injury. If people expose themselves to sunlight for the same periods in the same places as hitherto, increasingly more of them will suffer serious damage.

It is sensible, therefore, to reduce exposure to the sun; to cover up when the sun is at its most intense – particularly around midday and in the summer when it is least obstructed by the atmosphere. People with skins which are sensitive to sunlight should cover up in any event, and avoid any exposure which leaves their skin perceptibly hot and red afterwards. And parents should be particularly careful with children, whose skins are always more vulnerable.

People with dark skins are better protected naturally than those with fair skins; people with fair skins which tan easily, however, have some degree of protection once they are tanned. But anyone who wishes to enjoy the sun sensibly will aim to take it in far smaller doses over far longer periods. Whether it is already possible to feel the change is a moot point. Some people have however reported a prickly feeling in their skin, not previously experienced, when sunbathing in clear conditions in recent years.

Hazardous or not, many of us have not been willing to discipline our sunbathing in the past. Most of us live in places with no guaranteed sunshine; and we are mostly confined indoors at work for the greater part of the year whatever the conditions. When briefly free of that bondage we have tended to steer instinctively, and raw skinned, for the sunniest place we could find and to cook and baste ourselves for most of the time spent there. But we have judged the risk against known consequences in past conditions. Those conditions have gone and the assumptions of safety we based on them have gone with them. In addition, the conditions we now experience are on the slide.

We need to adapt our patterns of behaviour to match the change. But fortuitously, the greenhouse effect may well take some of the sting out of this need to adapt: we are likely to experience longer and more predictably sunny summers at home in future.

What, then, about the ozone in the air we breathe at ground level? Public authorities should warn us if ground-level ozone reaches dangerous levels. If they do, staying indoors will probably be sufficient protection for the majority; but anyone who has a chest or breathing problem ought now to avoid city-centre and other heavily polluted atmospheres on windless sunny days. Ozone builds up in such conditions and may harm vulnerable individuals even if below levels which are generally thought critical.

What the greenhouse effect may produce

We expect the climate to behave in a particular way at a particular time of year because that, more or less, is the way it has always behaved – during our own lives and those of our ancestors as far back as memory and records go. Our popular songs speak of April showers, as did Chaucer 600 years ago. But climate has only behaved in recognisably similar ways over long periods because the atmospheric system which deliver the weather to us have had broadly the same intensity and have followed broadly the same pattern during those periods. Weather may be almost infinitely variable on a day-to-day basis; but on average, clockwise-rotating high-pressure areas which deliver clear, dry, sunny, still weather, and anti-clockwise-rotating low-pressure areas which deliver stormy and wet or snowy weather, have turned up over more or less the same areas of land and sea at the same time for centuries.

The essential permanence of weather patterns is probably a basic function of climatic behaviour, and not only on earth. Over the several centuries since it became possible to observe the planet Jupiter, for example, its vast red spot has been noted in virtually the same position on the surface. Modern investigation has confirmed that that spot is a huge storm in the planet's atmosphere – one which has raged for centuries.

Our basic weather systems are therefore likely to stay as they are. But their power, and in consequence their influence on climate and weather, is likely to change radically as more energy is pumped into them.

It is the energy exchanged between relatively hot and relatively cold air masses when they collide which powers the climate. The cold side of the exchange is fed ultimately by the cold air masses over the polar ice-caps. Its intensity will remain more or less constant unless or until those ice-caps melt. But if more heat is fed into the hot side of the exchange because of the greenhouse effect, that heat will supercharge the system. Greater volumes of warmer moist air rising up within low-pressure systems will create far larger and more violent storm centres. Greater volumes of cool dry air, energy and moisture spent in storms will fall back to the surface through increasingly large and intense high-pressure systems. The end result will be weather conditions whose severity is extreme when measured against past experience worldwide.

Considered in the context of these basic mechanisms, we have to conclude that the greenhouse effect began to destabilise world climate long before recent times when meteorologists and climatologists announced that they were now convinced of coming climatic change. For two decades or more, reports of unprecedented climatic events – 'anomalous' in the guarded language of science – have multiplied worldwide. By definition, these events fell way outside the patterns which historic experience and records had accustomed people to expect. The climate is such that it will throw up local anomalies even when in a stable condition; but persistent anomalies on a global scale could only imply that the climate itself is changing.

This reminder is necessary for two reasons: first, the changes we face are almost certainly more deeply entrenched than their recent general acknowledgement suggests; second, much still depends on specialist interpretation, and different experts are still likely to confuse us by coming up with different conclusions for different reasons. In addition, events themselves may appear contradictory at local and regional levels. In the 1970s, for example, the northern hemisphere briefly became colder rather than warmer and all sorts of scenarios including an impending ice age were constructed on the fact. Globally, however, warming continued; and agencies such as the University of East Anglia's climatic research unit periodically reminded us of the fact.

Some argument about the greenhouse effect is therefore likely to endure until such time as changes are so fundamental that no one can ignore them. Dr Stephen Schneider of the American National Centre for Atmospheric Research has written that in his view, this should be within something like 10 years. In the meantime, unless or until people worldwide stop reporting weather conditions which transcend customary experience, our safest course is to accept the view now expressed by the majority of scientists concerned: that the climate is changing, that our actions are changing it, and that only different actions will restore stability.

What are the changes likely to be and how will they arrive in our own backyard?

Three basic weather patterns dominate the north Atlantic. First, there is a large anticyclonic high-pressure area centred over the Azores. Since around 1000 BC its intensity has been sufficient to block moist Atlantic air away from north Africa so that land fertile during the last ice age has become the Sahara Desert. Second, a constant stream of low-pressure storm centres follows, more or less, the route of the Gulf Stream up the east coast of North America and then across the north Atlantic from Iceland to Scandinavia. These depressions are fuelled by the relative warmth of the Gulf Stream beneath them. Finally, there is the mass of cold air over the Arctic Ocean, Greenland and the north Polar ice-cap.

When the cold polar air and water masses begin to extend southwards as winter approaches, they meet the depressions tracking the Gulf Stream. The extra energy exchanged, due to the sharpened contrast between the two, builds up these depressions into powerful storms and the autumn equinoctial gales result. The Azores anticyclone is shunted southwards by the energy in the north Atlantic storm centres and storms then dominate the north Atlantic and Western Europe.

Depending on their position, these storm centres may pump very cold conditions down from the Arctic, or very mild humid conditions up from further south in the Atlantic.

As winter advances and the Gulf Stream sheds its energy, its accompanying storms may lose their force. In past experience, this has often sufficed to allow very cold, dry continental weather conditions to feed in from the east. Then, as air masses again warm northwards from the equator in the spring, they impinge in turn on the receding Arctic air. The equinoctial gales traditionally associated with March were the product. When the Arctic air mass finally recedes in the late spring, the contrast between warm and cold again diminishes; the energy in low-pressure storm centres again reduces in consequence and, if we are lucky, the Azores anticyclone extends northwards bringing us hot, dry summers.

This a very abbreviated account of the manner in which long-established weather systems have contributed to our conception of the seasons.

The changes we are already experiencing are very much those which might be anticipated if more energy was introduced into that pattern. More heat in the atmosphere, the Gulf Stream and the storm systems which follow in its track would generate more violent storms which would continue longer into the winter until they came to dominate Western European weather between autumn and spring. Much of autumn and spring would coalesce with winter into one season which was mild, wet and periodically very stormy. Such tempestuous conditions would increasingly pump moist, warm air up into the Arctic, raising air and sea temperatures, but also increasing snowfall. Paradoxically, perhaps, these factors would initially combine to increase the volume of ice in land-based ice-fields, such as those covering Greenland, but to diminish the thickness of floating sea ice. Ultimately, however, if the major part of the sea ice melted a rapid warming would ensue which would also attack land-based ice-fields.

At the other end of the year, the Azores anticyclone would be likely to reach ever further and more frequently northwards. Late spring, summer and early autumn would also coalesce into one season – one which was increasingly hot and arid.

In the Arctic sea-ice is reported to have reduced in thickness by around 30 per cent over the last 10 years and southern Greenland is experiencing heavier snowfalls – to the extent that the increase in the permanent ice there has to be taken into account in calculating the effect on sea levels of ice melting elsewhere. We can judge whether the predictable consequences are showing up in temperate latitudes from our own experience.

The surge in temperatures during the climatic optimum between 6000 and 3000 BC most closely parallels that which seems likely to be an immediate result of the greenhouse effect, though events may move far more swiftly in our own time. Research into that period also hints at the conditions we can expect.

An analysis of pollen and plant remains shows that during the climatic optimum, many plant species flourished far north of the areas where we have so far been able to grow them. Those areas must have been significantly warmer and, for a period at least, the Arctic Ocean may well have been largely free of sea ice. Pollen analysis also reveals a sudden sharp decline in the number of trees.

Conventionally, that deforestation has been interpreted as reflecting the first impact of man and his farming, not least because layers of charcoal are often found in the sediments from which relevant pollen samples are taken. But that interpretation is less than satisfactory: people were still very few and far between during the climatic optimum and were hardly present in sufficient numbers to clear all the forest. On the other hand, storms of unprecedented ferocity in winter, followed by fires in fallen timber in unprecedented hot and dry summers, would have destroyed forests in a very short time. Our own experience in the last few years illustrates how it might happen; and the records from the climatic optimum add to the evidence which suggests that our recent experience is symptomatic of global warming.

The pollen record also shows that the number of elm trees fell drastically. We have had a similar experience. In the 1970s, Britain's elm trees were virtually wiped out by the Dutch elm disease fungus spread by a beetle. Yet both the beetle and the fungus have always been around, and researchers have suggested that some additional environmental factor was required to make the elm trees suddenly vulnerable. Evidence from the period of elm tree decline in the climatic optimum hints that rising temperature may have been the additional factor, both then and in our own time. In 1985, investigators found traces of the Dutch elm disease beetle in peat deposits taken from Hampstead Heath in London which dated to around 3800 BC.

Total rainfall was certainly lower during the climatic optimum than it has been since. Most of the peat bogs in north-west Europe have formed subsequent to that period, and many relics of the neolithic people who colonised north-west Europe during the climatic optimum have been found under peat.

Climatic change is one predicted consequence of the greenhouse effect; an accelerating increase in world sea levels is the other. Sea levels have risen steadily since the extreme of the last ice age, when they were as much as 100 metres or more below present levels, and there is some evidence that they rose even above present levels for a short period during the climatic optimum. They have certainly risen by around 15 cm since 1900, and increases in the 15–120 cm range are predicted over the next 50 years. That on its own is bad news for anyone who lives on land barely above sea level, or anyone who will be brought that much closer to storm-driven surges at high tides.

The danger in these predictions lies in the implicit suggestion that sea-level increases will occur in a measured and steady way, allowing plenty of time for avoiding action to be taken. If any large land-grounded ice-sheet, such as the Ross Ice Shelf in Antarctica, should suddenly experience an acceleration of its historically slow progress into the sea, world sea levels would rise immediately and substantially.

Global warming certainly increases the chance of such events, and the record of sea-level increases since the last ice age includes similar episodes. One occurred in around 3500 BC when ancient forests along the shoreline of Cardigan Bay in Wales were inundated. Their remains still sometimes reappear at low tides after storms have swept silt and sand off them.

Avoiding what the greenhouse effect may deliver

We cannot change what has already happened and is happening, although we may be able to prevent conditions from deteriorating still further. In previously temperate zones such as north-west Europe, we can still realistically aim to protect ourselves against existing climatic risks. The probability for the future is of mild but far more windy or severely windy and rainy weather in the winter; far more heat, sun and arid weather in the summer. It will not hurt us to consider the likely impact of such conditions on our lives.

Storm and flood exposure

It is obviously not a good time to look for a house which is exposed to the elements, if you do not already live in one. Most of us like the idea of a home with sweeping panoramic views; but if you can see out over the sea or a large tract of countryside, wild weather can come straight at you. Even if sea levels stay exactly where they are now, houses on low-lying land near tidal waters are liable to be flooded and damaged if severe storms combine with high tides. Those on low-lying land near rivers may be flooded after heavy rain, whether the rivers are tidal or not.

People who have already experienced such a misfortune will not need reminding that it is a possibility. What we all have to accept is the fact that it may now happen more frequently. After Britain experienced severe drought in 1976 and a hurricane in 1987, experts drew on historical evidence to conclude that neither was likely to recur for several hundred years. By 1990, both conditions had been repeated.

If you have so far escaped trouble in an exposed location, you should nevertheless encourage public authorities to review the quality of any measures previously considered adequate to protect your property. In any event, you will reduce the misery and chaos that follow when trouble strikes by ensuring that, as far as possible, your most vulnerable possessions are out of harm's way or can be swiftly moved. For example, even if your ground floor is at risk of flooding, the floors above may not be, and merely rearranging the way you live could save you serious losses in the event of a flood.

Trees

Whether your house is at high risk or not, it is worth taking some general precautions. If all trees are more likely to be blown down, it pays to cut back or remove any which are obviously rotten, or which might fall on and damage buildings or block access routes. Few of us enjoy losing or cutting back trees and most of us regard their conservation as environmentally important. Many trees are subject to tree preservation or other conservation orders for that reason and if this is the case for yours, you will have to obtain permission before they can be touched. But cutting out the topmost part of a tree will reduce the leverage generally in a storm and may save the tree as well as your property; and even if the whole tree has to be felled, it's better to lose its environmental benefit than to incur the environmental cost of having to repair damage caused by a fallen tree. From your own point of view, it is also better to have dealt with the tree in your own time than to have to compete for tree clearance and damage repair with thousands of other people after a major storm.

Property repair and maintenance

It is human nature to notice that something needs repair but to put off doing it. Past predictable weather conditions have tended to encourage such a relaxed attitude, but changing conditions may make it an expensive luxury. If roofs, walls or chimneys are already shaky it is better to have them repaired while everything is quiet than to join a long queue for more substantial repairs when a storm has blown them down altogether. Better also since you or someone dear to you could be injured when they come down. Insurance may meet the cost – at the price of higher future premiums. It will not save the additional resources needed for damage repair. It also makes sense to keep at hand tools and materials which you can use if things go wrong, even if only for temporary repairs – putty and a few spare sheets of glass, or a tarpaulin to keep the weather out, for example. No one who suffered from the hurricane winds which hit Britain in 1987 and 1990 will need reminding of how long they had to wait for essential repairs.

Emergency equipment

Many of us have lost the habit of keeping a few candles in the cupboard, new batteries for torches, spare batteries for portable radios, and something to cook on with enough fuel to keep it going. Even matches are hard to find in houses where no one smokes and nothing is burned. Many of us do not keep elementary first-aid equipment, or have elementary first-aid knowledge. Simple things like these may be important in the chaotic period which often follows immediately after some climatic disaster.

You may want to take more substantial precautions, as many people living in remote, isolated and exposed positions do as a matter of course. Wherever you live, a small stand-by generator can be a life-saver. Most central-heating systems have electrical pumps and controls, and no amount of fuel will keep you warm if there is no electricity to power them. A small generator will also suffice to keep your freezer, refrigerator and other light-load equipment going. But you do not need to invest in stand-by generators, chainsaws and CB radios merely to stave off the worst consequences of violent storm damage.

Transport and communications

It is also worth taking a moment to consider how the external essentials of ordinary life will continue if communications are severed. How would you cope if your roads were blocked and your telephone lines brought down? Even the most unlikely people sometimes fail to take account of these contingencies. It is rumoured, for example, that not so long ago a wild climatic frolic completely isolated an emergency services officer, and that much of one county's carefully thought-out emergency contingency planning ground to a halt because he was the only person who could direct it. Can you envisage anything which might bridge such a gap in your own life?

Drought

Even fine weather can become too much of a good thing. If summers become longer and drier, public water supplies planned on the assumption of regular rainfall will be vulnerable; most of those in the United Kingdom seem to have been so planned. Fire risks will also increase. The cost and environmental advantages of storing some of the rainwater from your roof have already been explored; but if dry summers, and with them water restrictions, become more common, stored water may mean that you have water for emergency or banned secondary uses which you would not otherwise have.

Conclusions

If predictions are borne out, the greenhouse and ozone effects are unlikely to make life too difficult, in the immediate future, for those of us who live in the higher latitudes of the northern hemisphere. Nor are they likely to produce results against which we cannot largely guard ourselves and our homes by taking sensible precautions. Indeed, the greenhouse effect may make our lives warmer and pleasanter and allow us to save energy previously used for heating. But that should not blind us to the fact that worldwide changing conditions may make water and food supplies far less reliable than they have been previously.

◆ 8 ◆

Checking Out Home Life

Introduction

This chapter serves as a check-list. It focuses on specific changes in the way we live at home which can save resources and environmental damage; and on steps we can take to minimise the impact on ourselves of the damage which has already occurred.

The previous chapters have surveyed the background logic for change and for taking avoiding action, since no one should advocate change without explaining the logic of it, even if that logic is universally known. But stating the logic for personal action is particularly important in the environmental field. Given the logic, individuals may well perceive, in their unique circumstances, environmentally helpful measures which no general survey could contemplate.

Several specific environmentally beneficial actions and activities have been offered by way of examples in the preceding chapters. These, together with others, are restated in this chapter in order to give a comprehensive summary, which is more helpful than one which includes numerous back references (even if there is as a result some repetition).

The guiding philosophy remains the same: everything we do to save resources and environmental damage is to the good, however trivial individual items may seem; and while our actions may at most involve large numbers of small contributions towards containing environmental damage, this will enable many of the large ones to take care of themselves.

Even if we are the only ones to adopt a particular course, our efforts will at least speak of our sincerity. That is also important:

110

there are still too many people who are happy to wring their hands in anguish over the environment on the grand scale, but are not willing to do anything about it on their own scale, where they can be effective. Example is essential. The greater the number of people that can be seen to be doing something, the greater the number likely to follow.

It is in our own interests that we in the richest nations, who consume most and pollute most, should take the lead. Several billion people living on earth have so little that they are bound to seek more. But we set the goalposts for what 'more' means. What will be left of anyone's environment if we continue along exactly the same horrifyingly damaging route, and hold it up as the example towards which billions claw their way? We pay lip service to the aspirations of newly liberated people in Eastern Europe and the Soviet Union who reach towards our way of life, yet our better living conditions exist only because we vent our wastes into parts of the environment which are far from home. We have to be able to demonstrate a way of life which is altogether less damaging; and, if we are sincere in arguing the benefits of freedom, we must be able to show that this better way of life can be achieved willingly.

The review of specific environmentally beneficial measures which follows is intended as much as a challenge to our ways of doing things as it is to prompt the adoption of some of these measures.

1. Permanent household structural features

Insulation

Once installed, insulation saves energy, cost and resources without further effort, helping to keep houses warm in cold weather and cool in hot weather. It is possible to do something to insulate the roof space and hot-water cylinder in virtually every house. The essentials are as much insulation as possible – at least 7 mm of mineral wool (or alternatives) – in roof insulation; lagging of water-pipes and apparatus which may suffer frost damage below the insulation; a proprietary hot-water cylinder jacket;

and an internal insulating lining on upstair ceilings if the roof space is not accessible.

Cavity walls can be insulated by pumping mineral wool or insulating foam into the cavity (this usually entails employing a contractor with specialised equipment). In the United Kingdom, most local council building departments keep lists of approved contractors. Ensuring that insulating building blocks are used in any new external walls is a simple way of insulating them from start.

Existing solid walls present greater problems if they are not thermally effective: a false internal wall with insulation or an insulating air space behind it may solve them; but anything hung on a cold external wall diminishes the area through which heat can be lost. The same goes for floors: insulation can be built into them if they have to be reconstructed, but floor coverings are a long-recognised practical answer.

Draught exclusion

Windows

If new windows have to be fitted, frames which are airtight and will stay airtight are desirable. Modern plastic (and often double-glazed) window units represent the ideal since they will not rot or corrode, and should not distort, but they are expensive. Hardwood timber frames are more resistant to future distortion and decay than softwood, but they, too, are costly. Double-glazing may be the only permanent cure for draughts from existing wooden frames; and sometimes the most cost-effective answer with new ones is to fit conventional low-cost wooden frames and then double-glaze inside them.

Double-glazing kits, available in most DIY stores, are an alternative to proprietary systems which are usually more costly. Many of the benefits of double-glazing can be achieved merely by sealing cracks with a suitable adhesive tape for the colder months of the year – but that is a tedious, impermanent and perhaps unattractive solution. Double-glazing saves significant energy if windows are otherwise draughty, but relatively little merely by reducing heat lost through glass. Blinds, shutters and curtains prevent warm internal air flowing against window glass and are as effective as double-glazing in preventing heat loss through glass – but only when they are closed or drawn.

External doors

External doors are a considerable source of draughts and heat loss. Replacing existing doors with modern, tight-fitting units is expensive, and on its own only effective when the doors are closed. French windows and patio doors are not normally opened in bad weather so new airtight doors, or double-glazing of existing ones, may suggest itself as a complete answer. However, if space allows (and it usually will) a less costly answer may be to enclose french windows or patio doors by erecting a proprietary lean-to aluminium greenhouse around their opening. It is not necessary to go full-tilt into expensive conservatories (for which planning permission may also be necessary). Apart from helping to solve draught and insulation problems and protecting existing doors from the weather, a lean-to greenhouse is likely to be useful in its own right. As long as its moisture levels are low, a greenhouse can also be used to supplement internal heating in fine weather: you just open the house connecting doors and let the heat in.

Airtight or not, if other external doors open straight into your house, there will be a significant heat loss every time they are opened. An enclosed porch on each external door – either built outside the house or constructed by partitioning off a space around the inner door – will save most of that heat loss. This formula is common in many older houses. Of course, much of the advantage disappears if both porch and house doors are open at the same time.

Necessary air flows

If you burn oil, gas, coal, wood or any other combustible fuel in any appliance in your house, it will require a good supply of air to function safely and efficiently. However airtight your house may be, the volume of air in it will usually be sufficient to supply appliances which have no flue, as long as they are not in small airtight rooms. But any appliance which sends combustion products up a flue reduces the air pressure in your house as it does so. This draws air in through any aperture which exists and creates an automatic draught between aperture and appliance. You can short-circuit those draughts by installing an air-pipe linking the closest point you can reach by the appliance to a ventilated under-floor area, or the exterior of your house. That will reduce the chances of draughts elsewhere, and ensure an adequate air flow if you have very efficient general draught exclusion.

Thermally effective window glass

It is now possible to buy specialised glass which lets heat in but prevents it from flowing out. Fitting it to suitable windows converts them into passive solar space heaters. But they will deliver more heat in the summer when it may not be needed than in the winter when it is. Some large buildings have been specifically designed to use this form of space heating, but the glass is usually only part of a complex air-conditioning system. The glass on its own has limited practicality as a source of domestic energy.

Timber protection

All timber is at risk of attack by fungus and woodworm – window frames in particular – and the interests of conservation are served if any accessible existing timber is treated in situ and all new timber treated before it is fixed. Preserving timber saves trees as well as cash. Steps taken to exclude draughts should never include the blocking of air-bricks or ventilation spaces which are necessary to stave off damp and decay in timber.

2. Heating appliances

The need for some domestic space and water heating is not likely to disappear, however effective insulation and draught exclusion may be. The source of that heat may be conventional, innovatory, or it may involve a combination of the two.

Conventional heating

Electricity should be avoided for space and water heating. You will have the benefit of as much as 85 per cent of the energy produced by burning solid fuel, oil or gas in a well-designed modern domestic appliance (the modern gas condensing burner is a particular example) which is connected to an appropriate and properly balanced chimney or flue. You will only have between 35 per cent and 45 per cent of the benefit of the same fuel burned in a power station if you heat with electricity.

Chimneys and flues

Proper balancing of chimneys and flues is important. High winds set up powerful suction forces, an effect most obvious in the way open fires and solid fuel appliances burn more fiercely and lose more heat up the chimney in windy conditions. A simple flue balancer admits air to the flue and reduces excessive suction: this saves both heat and fuel wastage.

If you have to install a new flue, modern proprietary sectional insulated stainless steel systems are usually the cheapest. If you have room to run a flue of this type up inside your house and out through the roof, you can recover some of the flue heat for internal space heating. Heat from the flue gases passing up such systems penetrates through their outer casing at safe levels.

Heat pumps

Electricity may be an efficient source of space and water heating if used to drive a heat pump. Heat pumps circulate a heat transfer gas through low-level heat sources in the external environment and concentrate them by compression (a bicycle pump becomes hot when used by the same process). Depending on the amount of heat present in the external source – soil, water or air – the usable heat produced by a heat pump may be two, three, four or more times that which would be yielded merely by burning the electricity required to drive the pump. But heat pump installations are expensive.

Solar panels

If you install solar panels they may, even in northern latitudes, produce enough energy to heat the main part of your domestic hot water between, say, the middle of April and the middle of September each year. This allows oil, gas or solid fuel appliances to be turned off. However, solar panels may not suffice even in that period if the sky is overcast. Relying on solar water heating topped up by sparing, intermittent use of an electric water heater may still be efficient overall in energy terms. But solar panels require careful cost-benefit comparisons if you plan to install them from scratch and you don't plan to do this yourself. The value of the energy which can be saved during the likely operating life of some proprietary systems is sometimes less than the cost of their installation.

Other natural sources

You may be able to generate your own electricity by wind or water power if your property is suitably sited. But for the reasons outlined in Chapter 2, these are not options available to most people (see pages 31–2).

3. Movable household equipment

Everything in our houses reflects resources used and environmental harm caused somewhere in the course of manufacture and delivery to us. All that is past history once an article has been acquired; however, its future use involves further damage if it is active equipment which requires energy or any other resource to function.

We can aim to minimise the additional damage caused by using active equipment. All electrical equipment, of course, has its wattage rating stamped on it somewhere. If you run an appliance rated at 1000 watts (or several which total that amount) for an hour, you consume 1kWh of electricity – one unit as charged in the United Kingdom.

Kitchen appliances

Hot plates and gas rings
Cooking on an open hob, hot plate, gas or electric ring is wasteful since a great deal of the heat burned rises up past the pan. Cooking in a pan without a lid on is even more wasteful, since heat is lost additionally from the contents. Some cooking requires these methods, but a great deal does not: for example, eggs can be soft boiled in five minutes from the time they are put into boiling water in a pan with a lid on it, even if the heat is switched off as soon as the water is brought back to the boil. Left longer, they hard boil. People have been known to aim for even greater efficiency by boiling eggs in electric kettles.

Pressure cookers
On open rings, pressure cookers are more efficient than pans with lids, since pressurised steam cooks food far more quickly.

Electric element heated appliances
Enclosed appliances with built-in electric heating elements – often also insulated and thermostatically controlled – are generally more efficient than any pan or kettle on an open ring or hot plate. More of the heat created is contained within them and so in addition are cooking smells.

Enclosed deep fryers, cooking pans, electric kettles and coffee pots or percolators with built-in electric elements are therefore preferable to open-ring cooking, if you have the means to acquire them. Some of these appliances use less energy than an open ring or hot plate. Even those with similar or higher energy ratings (2.4 to 3 kW electric kettles for example) save energy by doing the job far more quickly. Boiling water in an electric kettle and then pouring it on to something which has to be boiled in a pan on an open ring or hot plate will also save energy: the water is brought to the boil more efficiently in the kettle than in the pan.

Conventional ovens
Conventional ovens – gas, oil, electric or solid fuel – are far less

efficient than the microwave alternative, even if well insulated and thermostatically controlled. Electric ovens are generally rated in the 3000–5000-watt range and those heated by other fuels require comparable energy inputs. Microwave ovens cook faster and may be rated at 750 watts or less. If your oven is hot all the time, as it will be if you have a multi-purpose stove of the AGA–Rayburn type, it obviously makes sense to use it for all cooking which can be done at the normal running temperature of your oven. But if you have to raise normal oven temperature significantly before you cook, you are likely to burn more energy as you raise it than if you used a conventional oven. Higher than normal temperatures and frequent temperature changes will also significantly shorten the life of firebricks and exposed metal parts.

Microwave ovens

Radio waves in the radar waveband supply the cooking energy used inside the shielded volume of microwave ovens. Those waves penetrate and heat food from the inside by vibrating the molecules, particularly large fat, sugar and water molecules. Because a microwave oven is essentially a sophisticated piece of electronic radio equipment, it uses far less power than a conventional oven in which energy has to be burned to produce crude heat. But microwave ovens which additionally contain a heating element to produce a conventional baked result will consume just as much electricity as a comparable electric oven, when the heating element is used.

Oven-proof glass casseroles (with glass lids) are ideal for microwave cooking. A stock of sizes sufficient to take everything from chickens and joints of meat down to small portions of fruit or vegetables saves any need for makeshift containers covered by plastic film – which can also lead to the risk of chemical food contamination.

Apart from energy advantages, when compared with other cooking methods microwave cooking preserves far more of the flavour and nutritional value of fresh food, particularly that in fruit and vegetables. Far shorter cooking times and the far smaller volume of cooking water required achieve that result.

Deep freezers, convenience foods and microwaves

If you have a deep freezer you can prepare your own convenience foods, avoiding both subsequent contamination and any excess use of salts. When cooking, you can cook more than you need for immediate consumption (which itself is economical in time and resources), and freeze the surplus immediately in suitable portions. Fresh fruit and many fresh vegetables can be frozen for later use whether they require pre-cooking or not. A microwave oven resurrects these convenience foods in perfect condition almost instantaneously.

Manufactured pre-packed convenience foods use more resources, and not only for packing. Recent research suggests that they may also be inherently dangerous if later put in the microwave as intended. Manufacturers use several different salts to preserve convenience foods and enhance their appearance and flavour. Research at Leeds University suggests that these salts prevent microwaves from penetrating food which contains them, even if the food is microwaved for recommended periods. The surface of the food is heated but its interior remains cold. Any salmonellae, listeria or other harmful bacteria which have penetrated the food between manufacture and consumption are not then killed off by cooking.

Refrigerators

Refrigerators usually have a long operational life but many refrigerators (and freezers) presently in use are inadequately insulated and wastefully designed. If you have to buy a new one, both you and the environment will benefit if you first ask for details of running costs and buy the one with the lowest available. Many fridges now on the market burn between 2 and 3kWh (units) of electricity a year for each litre of space in them. The best designs may reduce consumption 10 times, down to 0.4 to 0.2kWh a litre.

Design apart, the way you use a refrigerator matters. Energy is wasted when the door is opened, and – open or closed – if ice builds up round the ice-box. Ice is an effective insulator: ice round ice-boxes slows down the rate at which the mechanism will extract heat and increases the energy needed to extract it.

Freezers
The points made about design and need for care in purchasing with regard to refrigerators apply equally to freezers. Again, energy is wasted when a freezer door is opened, whatever the design. But far more energy is wasted when you open an upright freezer than a chest freezer, because more expensively generated cold air falls out of the former each time the door is opened. Even if running costs do not not matter, anyone concerned for the environment will opt for a chest freezer if space allows – and for the biggest he or she can accommodate and keep reasonably full. The resource, running and, usually, cash cost per litre of space reduce as the size of the freezer grows, provided it is kept well stocked. But freezers also use more energy if ice is allowed to build up on their walls.

Scrapping refrigerators and freezers. Virtually all existing refrigerators and freezers contain CFCs – the ozone-destroying chlorofluorocarbon gases – in their sealed cooling circuits. Some time will elapse before cooling equipment is available that can use the new CFC substitutes which will not imperil high-level ozone (but may still have a greenhouse effect 4000 to 6000 times that of carbon dioxide). If you have to scrap existing cooling equipment, check to make sure that it goes to a supplier or tip where the coolant gases will be drained off and safely contained. If equipment is traded in or dumped without thought its heat exchange circuits may be smashed open and the gases released to the atmosphere.

Dishwashing machines and the Victorian alternative
Dishwashing machines are convenient. But if you had to select the household appliance which causes the most unnecessary harm to the environment for the benefit it gives, the automatic dishwasher would probably be the one. The environmental damage inherent in the manufacture of dishwashers including resources used is subsequently multiplied many times over by the energy needed to drive them; the volume of fresh water which passes through them; the abrasive additives which have to be put into them; and the regularity with which they are used.

And for what? More than 100 years ago the Victorians

systematised the washing-up process very satisfactorily with two sinks and a dishrack. The huge kitchens of vast Victorian country houses, in which the amount of washing-up from one meal alone was often far and above that we have to wash in a week, had two cavernous sinks. Dishes and utensils were washed first in hot water to which soap and washing soda were added; rinsed in clean cold water in the second; and drained and dried naturally in the dishrack. The Victorians rinsed in cold water because hot water was not on tap; cold utensils take longer than hot ones to dry so they needed very large dishracks.

The essence of this simple, effective, efficient and hygienic system often seems to have been forgotten over the years as kitchens have been scaled down to their modern size, and the quantity of washing-up has been scaled down with them. But although washing-up is a chore whatever the method – and you still have to wash many cooking vessels by hand even if you possess a dishwasher – the old method is far kinder to the environment and can be as swift, efficient, and hygienic as any automatic dishwasher.

You need two ordinary washing-up bowls and an ordinary dish and cutlery drainer. Wash in warm water in the first, using whatever washing-up substance you choose; but unlike in Victorian kitchens, dishes should be rinsed in very hot water in the second. The heat absorbed in the rinse dries everything almost immediately you fish it out and put it in the drainer. That makes it very easy to clear the decks. To be really friendly to the environment you will use washing soda to shift any grease (see Appendix on pages 138–9) and an ordinary soap, not a modern detergent, to suspend it. And, if you have only one bowl, you can still use the same method: wash first, refill the bowl with hot rinsing water, and pass everything through the rinse.

As modified, the old system removes any traces of cleaning substances; spares any need to wipe or dry and any risk of spreading bacteria lurking in any cloth; and minimises waste and harm to the environment. Twelve litres of water do the same job as 25–35 litres in a dishwasher; using little more effort than stacking and unstacking a dishwasher you save perhaps 3000 watts of electricity.

Other appliances

Automatic washing-machines

Automatic washing-machines – particularly those which offer half washes for smaller quantities – have environmental advantages over virtually all their alternatives, and these in addition to their labour-saving virtues. The modern washing-machine will wash larger quantities of clothes with smaller quantities of water than any manual alternative. Using cold water and modern low-temperature washing powders (preferably those that are environmentally friendly, of course) they save energy which more than offsets that used to drive them. The centrifugal force of the high-speed spin available in virtually all washing-machines extracts far more water from clothes than was ever possible by wringing out by hand or with a mangle. This saves time and any energy needed afterwards for drying.

Tumbler-driers

If the modern washing-machine is an environmental plus, the tumbler-drier is not. The motor, fan and heating element in a drier may together be rated at 3000 watts or more, and in the end a tumbler-drier only does the same job as a clothes rack in a warm place, and rather less than an outside washing line. Clothes dried in the fresh air usually dry fresh and soft without any of the advertised washing and softening additive.

Both we and the environment could do without tumbler-driers altogether and we should only use them as a last resort.

Electric space heaters

Fan heaters, convection heaters, electrically heated radiators, ordinary electric fires, and even night storage heaters, for all the tariff advantages offered with them, are very heavy electricity users. They may be handy in emergency, but should if possible be strictly avoided for regular use.

In some households, this will mean putting them out of sight since they are so convenient to use and other family members may not share your concern with the environment.

122

Electric lights

One electric light bulb does not use much electricity. Several switched on together soon gallop through it. The long-life miniature neon tube bulbs described on page 47 produce the same amount of light as conventional bulbs for very much less electricity. Switching off unnecessary lights is advisable whatever lamps are used; but remembering to do it consistently is difficult. Fitting low-consumption lamps, if only in the outlets most frequently in use, does most of the job automatically.

Vacuum-cleaners

It may be a false economy to choose a low-powered vacuum-cleaner in preference to a high-powered one. The essential component of a vacuum-cleaner is its fan which is driven by an electric motor. The more powerful the motor, the greater the suction for a given amount of motor strain; and wear and tear are significant since vacuum-cleaners are used frequently. A high-powered cleaner will use more energy than a low-powered one while it is running; but it is likely to do the job in a shorter time and the amount of electricity used by both may be very much the same. Because of motor strain, a high-powered cleaner may also last longer than a low-powered one. Added together, these factors are likely to mean that overall, high-powered machines use less resources and energy than low-powered ones. For domestic purposes, a cleaner rated at 1000 watts or more is likely to be a much better environmental bet than one between 200 and 300 watts.

Electric irons

The conventional electric flat iron is usually rated at 1000 watts; these irons deliver a very high temperature over a small area, producing a sharp, crisp result in the clothes which are ironed. This is, however, achieved at the price of fabric damage which shortens the life of clothes. Ironing with flat irons without steam devices is also hard work because you have to lean over and press down the iron. Rotary irons or steam presses are a better alternative.

Rotary irons and steam presses

Modern rotary irons and steam presses generally have a higher power rating than flat irons – perhaps 1200 watts for a rotary iron. But they deliver heat to clothes far more evenly through a larger blade or heated element and with far less damage to fabric. Ironing with this type of equipment is significantly faster than with a flat iron once you are used to it, and as with vacuum-cleaners, speed can offset the extra energy requirement. It is also less tiring since pressure is applied to clothes by leverage, typically through a cable link to a pedal. Rotary irons and steam presses save energy, labour, time and excessive fabric damage.

Electronic equipment

Televisions, radios, audio equipment, computers and other electronic equipment (including microwave ovens) use very little electricity. Transistors and micro-circuits powered by mains electricity take up only a fraction of the power and resources used by the heated valves in older equipment. In addition, the range and quality of electronic equipment is now such that arguably we can have entertainment – and education – in our own own homes which equals standards available anywhere, and the resources and energy costs of travelling elsewhere to find it are saved. Indeed, we can often hear or see more with electronic equipment than we could if we travelled to find a live presentation or performance.

Battery-powered equipment and transformers

Battery-powered electrical and electronic equipment has a voracious appetite for resources – and cash. Batteries are a useful emergency standby; but they are seldom essential for day-to-day use, and the waste and pollution which starts with their manufacture does not end when they are spent and disposed of. Many highly rated modern batteries contain toxic metals, such as cadmium, and this applies also to built-in long-life rechargeable batteries. In addition, scrapped batteries add to toxic pollution.

Even equipment without a built-in mains electricity connection usually has a connector for mains power from a transformer. Small transformers are cheap – often little more than two or three times the cost of one battery replacement. Transformers with multi-purpose bayonet connectors are generally available, so one transformer may do for virtually any appliance. Transformers save resources and cost and should be used instead of batteries as far as possible. Small appliances, such as calculators, may be battery or solar (light) powered; those powered by light are obviously preferable if either will do the job.

Information technology equipment

Electronic information technology equipment – telephone, fax, computers, computer printers and modems – opens the door to substantial resource savings, especially if you can do a significant part of your work at home avoiding the need to travel to a separate workplace. That scenario is considered in detail in on pages 71–4. Having such equipment at home may help you to familiarise yourself with it, and so pave the way towards such a pattern of work. Unless you have that opportunity or are working towards it, however, the resources used to manufacture any information technology equipment you acquire are likely to represent a total loss both to you and the environment.

4. Household waste

Solid waste and liquid waste require separate consideration.

Solid waste

Recycling

Recycling starts at home. Any wrapping, package or container which will save you from having to buy or acquire something else for the same job should be preserved and re-used. Virtually every household quickly accumulates enough plastic carrier bags for all future shopping; and ordinary retail purchases come with enough plastic and other containers to meet all future needs for storing dry goods – sugar, salt, flour, dried fruit, flour and cereals – and foods to be kept in a larder, refrigerator or freezer.

All those universal lidded plastic boxes and containers have further uses such as storing stock and convenience foods in the freezer; for pins, nails and screws; for plants in the garden or greenhouse. Tea leaves and coffee grounds, useful as soil additives in a garden or window-box and useless if poured down the drain, can first be collected in a plastic box in the cupboard under the sink. Even a used tea bag can be recycled as a drainage filter under the soil at the bottom of a plant-pot.

Households have long treasured jam and other glass jars for stores and preserves. The plastics which have displaced so many of them are no less useful.

Sorting waste such as paper, aluminium cans and bottles for general recycling may be your next priority, but only if you have a collection depot handy. If you have to take your car out specially to reach a recycling depot, you are likely to burn more energy – and cause more environmental damage – than if you burn your waste or put it out for refuse collection.

The first priority for food wastes is to recover anything which we or our animals can reasonably consume. The most neglected end of that exercise is boiling up food residues to produce stock liquors and storing these for future soups, casseroles and general cooking uses. Domestic animals too can help dispose of leftovers, and the garden compost heap should be the destination for all vegetable matter.

Solid waste which will not recycle
Apart from plastics and any other substance which releases toxic gases as well as smoke and carbon oxides when burnt, anything left which can be burned should be burned. Burning on an open fire or in a garden incinerator is less harmful to the environment than decay in a council landfill tip. Only what then remains should go into the refuse bag for collection – ash, and inert and undegradable substances.

Liquid waste

Drinking water
Drinking water costs resources; restricting its use saves them. A shower uses less water than a bath; washing-up by hand uses less than a dishwasher; a loo cistern with a water-filled plastic bottle in it uses less than one without (see page 63); a watering-can for the garden or for rinsing the car uses less than a hose or

sprinkler; taps, pipes or overflows which do not drip or leak use less (sometimes far less) than those which do.

Recycling water

Rainwater from the roof is the most obvious target for recycling. Some of it can be collected in a suitable rainwater butt or other tank and subsequently used in the garden or greenhouse – or for some other purpose for which purified drinking water is either unnecessary or undesirable. Trace chemicals in drinking water are harmful to some plants. Soaps, detergents and grease (but not bleach) will not cause any harm if bath or washing-up water is used again in a garden, though they may should not be poured regularly on plants in pots. If you have a water meter or are subject to restrictions on the use of water, you may be re-using domestic waste water anyway in times of drought: but only those who are truly dedicated to the environment will do this as a matter of course.

Water down the drain

Reducing the volume of water you send down the drain is one part of the environmental concern, not least because that water usually starts off as purified drinking water; avoiding the addition of anything to that water which may subsequently be harmful to the general environment is the other. At best it costs extra resources to remove harmful additives during any subsequent sewage treatment; but once introduced most additives cannot be removed.

If it can be avoided, insoluble solids such as disposable nappies, condoms, tampons and sanitary towels should not go down the drain. Burn them or wrap them in bags recycled from general shopping and put them out for refuse collection. Soap, washing soda (see Appendix on pages 138–9) and other benign cleaning substances should be used rather than bleach and detergents; detergents which do not contain phosphates for water softening and foaming agents to produce a lather are preferable to those which do.

These considerations are particularly important if your foul drainage goes into a septic tank. Septic tanks only work properly if naturally occurring anaerobic bacteria thrive in them. Solids and chemicals which make bulk sewage treatment more difficult and cause other damage if poured down main sewers will clog the workings of a septic tank altogether. A dedicated environmentalist who is not squeamish and keeps a septic tank in good condition could even consider using it to supplement his garden fertiliser. This involves opening the tank's inspection hatch periodically, cutting out part of the floating crust of digesting solid matter on the surface, and using it in the same way as any other manure. However, this is not something to be attempted without great care; anyone who falls into a septic tank is likely to drown in a particularly nasty way.

5. Gardens

Vegetables, herbs, fruit and flowers

Any piece of ground on which plants can be grown or productive animals kept has a potential either for environmental benefit and resource saving, or for further damage and waste. If you apply your spare time and energy to food production in a garden or allotment, you reduce the demand on general resources; you are able to control what chemicals are used and generally benefit your family with fresher, more palatable food. If, on the other hand, you devote time, energy, space and resources only to grass and flowers, you merely add to the sum total of resource depletion and waste.

This is not to say that every inch of a garden should be turned over to potatoes and other vegetables. Aesthetic considerations apart, some flowers – African marigolds, for example – protect crops grown near them against insect pests, and knowledgeable gardeners are aware of this. In addition, many gardens have an odd corner which is suitable for flowers – particularly perennials, such as spring bulbs – and unsuitable for anything else; and some food-producing plants, such as herbs and fruit trees, are also very attractive. Why grow an ornamental cherry tree when an apple, pear, peach, vine, loganberry or plum will flower equally attractively and be far more fruitful? Why grow privet hedges when many thorny fruit trees will serve equally well?

The smallest gardens will produce something, and many useful herbs grow very well in window-boxes. The more land you have, however, the greater your scope for productivity.

Greenhouses

Even a cold-frame or small greenhouse widens the range of plants which can be home grown. Under glass, summer hardy plants can be brought on earlier for later open planting; and even without heating, tomatoes, cucumbers, melons, peppers and dwarf fruit trees in pots (lemon, peach, nectarine and fig are examples) which might not survive at all in the open will flourish.

A lean-to greenhouse built on to french windows or patio doors does double duty, protecting, insulating and draught-proofing the doors as well as encouraging plant growth. Such a greenhouse may even serve to boost house space heating in sunny weather: you simply open the house doors and let the heat in. But moisture will come in too if humidity levels are high, as they will be if plants have recently been watered.

Greenhouses need adequate balanced ventilation; but if you fit proprietary temperature-driven window-openers, these will do the job automatically. Greenhouses built over a solid flagged or concrete base (with drain holes), and with soil beds perhaps 25 cm deep laid on that base, need less water and need and lose less soil nutrient than those resting on soil. It is also much easier to dig in compost or manure and dig over greenhouse beds if they are formed on a hard base. You can soon build up a soil quality equal to any proprietary growing bag – and avoid the need for buying one. An extendable window-cleaning brush is useful for cleaning greenhouse glass, as it is for cleaning house windows.

Livestock

Pet or semi-domesticated animals can also play a useful role. Many animals help by recycling food and garden waste into manure. If you keep hens in large numbers and they are allowed to roam free, they will cause plant damage (they are also at risk from predators); and you will have to supplement their food significantly with bought-in supplies if you want them to lay well. However, one or two hens – bantams are a favourite –

can be kept in a very small space and your meat and vegetable kitchen waste will suffice for most of their feed. You will not be overwhelmed with the eggs laid by a couple of hens, but you will know where they have come from and how they have been produced.

If you have space and the inclination to keep bees, your fruiting plants and trees which require pollination will yield better, and you will have the prospect of honey as a bonus. With more space (and ambition, perhaps) you can extend the range of your produce to include meat or dairy produce from a couple of goats, sheep or a cow. Large animals will recycle far more waste vegetable matter into valuable garden manure; but any animal which needs daily attention restricts your family's mobility.

6. Transport

In an ideal, environmentally concerned world, people would walk, cycle, paddle their own canoes, be propelled by their own animals or, at worst, use public transport. This is still the way in which three-quarters of the people on earth live. If all five billion of the world's inhabitants used aircraft, motor and other vehicles as we do, however, any environment worth saving would already have perished – taking us along with it.

Our choices generally include private cars. We should reduce their use to a minimum. Unleaded petrol merely solves one localised environmental problem; it does nothing to reduce the health hazards of fuel combustion products or their greenhouse and ozone gas effects. During the Second World War, the Central Office of Information regular advertised the question: 'Is your journey really necessary?' That question is even more relevant now that our abuse of the environment is swiftly giving rise to the most perilous enemy we have ever faced. No official is yet posing the question, or denying us options if we ignore it. But private motoring is a significant source of atmospheric pollution. Other gases apart, one-fifth of the carbon dioxide released in Britain comes from vehicle exhausts.

We have inherited a compulsion towards personal mobility from a past in which travelling was virtually the only means of communication with other people. Despite all the alternatives which now exist, that compulsion survives. But if we continue to yield to it without restraint, it alone may bring us to our knees.

Our literary tradition includes accounts of great journeys made by a handful of privileged, and sometimes brave, individuals. Our age has brought the ends of the earth within hours of where we are, and has taken most of the sting out of reaching them, but the environment is paying a fearful price for our passion to visit more distant places – and that goes as much for the next town as it does for Tashkent or Samarkand.

The environmental damage to which all this is contributing now reaches ever more deeply into our own backyards. None of us can now afford to ignore the fact that there is a connection between that damage and the journeys we make to distant places, however attractive those journeys may be.

We need to balance every attractive aspect of mobility against its environmental cost and against possible alternatives: the virtues of the small car using less fuel, against the 'status' of the big car which uses more; the appropriateness of travelling by bus or train, against the dismissive 'Oh no, I go by car'; the significance of holidays closer to home, against the greater resources used and pollution caused when we reach for far away places.

7. Appliances, tools and equipment

Appliances, tools and other articles are now available for virtually every purpose imaginable, but whole industries are nonetheless devoted to dreaming up yet more. Some improve our ability to provide, maintain or repair services or articles which would cost more in resources if we purchased the alternative. To that limited extent they are kind, rather than unkind, to the environment.

But much of this merchandise is little more than a gimmick; and it is often the case that the more vigorously it is advertised the more gimmicky it is. None of us is likely to succeed all the time in avoiding gimmicks and very few of us can look around our homes without finding several already tucked uselessly away in corners. These are personal monuments to our past assaults on the resources of the earth and its environment, and even supposedly environmentally friendly articles are beginning to number among them.

We can at least reduce the number we add to them in the future. Simple questions should be asked before we buy: do we already have something which is still doing the same or a similar job adequately? Is it a job which needs doing? Will having this gadget make it possible for us to save a future purchase which will cost more to buy, maintain and run? If it will merely save time and labour, will we use that time and labour to save more than its cost? Cash cost and benefit do not give the total measure of resource cost and environmental damage (or benefit), but they supply the most accurate measure to hand.

8. Work, time and energy

General

We all need to relax, rest and exercise in order to remain healthy. Most of the rest we need comes from sleep and in that we are responding to the demands of our own constitution: our personal environmental 'fail-safe' system decides when and for how long we need to sleep.

For practical purposes, our lives consist of the periods when we are not asleep – and that makes them rather shorter than the span between the moment when we are born and the moment when we die. Within that span, we have to accommodate work. The trouble is that we have allowed work to become synonymous with virtue: a person who works, still more one who works hard, is good; a person who does not work is bad. As a result, any activity which can be labelled as work tends to be accepted as unquestioningly good.

Increasingly, this is not so, either for us or for our environment. The contradictions are most obvious in those industries which have been kept going, virtuously providing people with work, when the absence of any sufficient demand for their product has meant that they have consistently turned in losses – sometimes staggering losses. By every measure – money, human skill, energy, resources and environmental pollution – their real product has been waste.

Exactly the same can happen at the individual level. Should time spent earning £1000 in a week be a matter of pride if an individual earning it must then pay someone else £1000 to do a job which he could do himself in less time and at far less cost in resources? As a very simple example, how many can earn enough to pay even the labour cost of employing someone to paint their house in the time it would take them to paint it themselves?

The work ethic

When it comes to saving waste, even the work ethic needs review. We live in a money economy and are not likely to live otherwise, so we all need some income. But beyond a certain point, time which we might use productively ourselves may be of greater value to us – and to the environment – than time, and the cash it yields, which is committed to others. Piling up income and burning resources in the process may itself be environmentally destructive.

Travel to work

If this is true for time and resources specifically committed to work, it is still more true for those spent in travel to and from work when time, energy and resources are generally all wasted. Some bold spirits insist that they work productively while they are travelling. Indeed, some protest that this is when they do their best work (although this suggests that they would be far more productive if they never set off in the first place!).

The environmental burden imposed by millions in daily transit to work requires all of us to consider the alternatives in modern technology discussed more fully on pages 71–4.

Free time

Free time exists outside that committed to work and to moving back and forth at its command. Its quantity is increasing as technology impinges on work, usually with environmental advantages. Technology has reduced the physical demands of work; more and more of us must burn physical energy in our spare time if only because our health and welfare demand it.

Healthwise there is little to choose between the different types of physical activity, productive or otherwise. But the environment gains if we choose activities which yield useful goods or services, and loses if we do not.

To say that is not to insist that everyone should immediately substitute gardening, building, property maintenance or any other productive activity for jogging, squash, golf, rowing or participating in any other sport; or that they should always walk or cycle rather than use motorised transport. Still less is it to criticise unproductive activity among people whose home environment offers few alternatives, save perhaps that of climbing stairs rather than using a lift.

But anyone who has the choice between spare-time activities which are productive and save resources, and those which are not and which further consume them, should reflect on the environmental consequences of the balance they maintain between the two.

9. Ozone effects

Proportions of ozone are increasing at ground level and decreasing in the high atmosphere. If we are concerned for our health and welfare, we must all start taking precautions beyond those to which we are accustomed. Anyone with respiratory problems should avoid congested urban areas, and anywhere subject to significant atmospheric pollution, in clear, still, sunny weather when ozone levels may rise. We should reflect additionally on the wisdom of driving into such conditions, since ozone is harmful to all life.

The increasing damage to the ozone layer in the upper atmosphere and the extra ultra-violet radiation reaching the earth's surface as a result implies a growing need for people to modify their sun-bathing habits: to avoid over-exposure leading to red and tender skin; to harden off the skin adequately by sun-bathing for shorter periods in the day, over a greater number of days than hitherto; and to exercise particular care over children and anyone else with a sensitive skin.

Lotions which genuinely mask ultra-violet radiation may protect, but they only work if they slow down the rate at which the skin tans significantly, since it is the radiation which causes the tan. Lotions which merely ease discomfort do not protect: the damage is done if the discomfort exists.

10. Greenhouse effects

The warming of the earth's atmosphere threatens to produce more extreme weather conditions more frequently: heat and drought, as well as storm, tempest and flood.

It will pay us, and the environment, to collect and retain rain water for uses for which pure water is not necessary; to remedy structural defects which make our houses more vulnerable to being ripped open in violent weather; to store articles particularly sensitive to water damage sensibly if there is a flood risk; to top or remove trees which would cause damage or injury if felled by a storm; to clear potentially inflammable undergrowth round our houses; and to review how we might keep the basic essentials of life going if public supplies, services or communications fail.

We have already experienced extreme weather conditions which have left people without food, water, heat, light, shelter, communications, transport, first aid or the benefit of emergency services. The information emerging about the greenhouse effect suggests that such experiences will not be unique in our lives.

9

Conclusions

There are soft, and less soft options when it comes to the environment. The soft option is to buy goods with green labels on them, but otherwise continue exactly as before; to protest and worry about the actions of others which seem to threaten the environment on the grand scale, but do nothing to change our own; to participate in grand schemes to create, plant or preserve a few trees here, a few blades of grass there, a hedgerow down one side of a road, or a tunnel for frogs or hedgehogs down the other, and then go comfortably home to exactly the same way of life.

There is good in all of these things and others like them; but their effect is at best cosmetic. It is unlikely to achieve anything more than a few embarrassed islands in a world turned increasingly into wilderness by continued population growth and the ever more insatiable demand upon resources and goods.

The less soft option is to face up to the truth about the driving force behind all these concerns: to acknowledge that the machine is not driven by those who cause or threaten damage on the vast scale, but by each and every one of us who demands or consumes the product of that damage on the small scale. For example, elephants would roam the spaces still left for them in Africa with relative impunity if no one had bought those tiny attractive ivory carvings.

Individually, we are judge and jury of what is happening to our environment. We are also the accused. We will share the penalty if we judge wrongly; but that will not absolve us of the crime of which we will be guilty if we destroy others, and other species, who are helpless passengers on the vehicle we are driving.

The simplest and most straightforward message is to spend less, use less, waste less, pollute less – even earn less. The world would not be at any risk at all (though we would be) if we could take no more out of it than our own physical strength allows.

Between that extreme and the other at which we now stand there are positions from which we might aim to keep the essence of our modern lives without throwing the baby out with the bathwater. But to reach those positions we need concerted action to rein back consumption. The world does not have the time, the resources or the will to achieve anything like enough merely by cleaning up production. When it comes to consumption, however, we can each achieve a great deal.

This study does not contain a comprehensive and all-embracing blueprint for that exercise, but it does include some specific recommendations, and it also sets out quite deliberately to argue their logic. For if the logic is accepted and applied, people will find additional measures which they can adopt in their special circumstances.

The essence of the damage we are inflicting on the world, and the consequences which increasingly haunt us, lies in what we are taking out of it and what we expect to take out of it. None of us is free of guilt in this process and each of us can do something to help arrest it. If enough of the people in the world's richest countries are prepared to face this challenge and to act upon it, the processes of environmental decay can be contained and containing them will not hurt anyone too much.

Appendix
Washing Soda and Its Uses

Cautions
Soda may discolour some types of aluminium. Like all cleaning substances it should be kept out of reach of children, should not be drunk, and it is best to wear gloves when using it in strong solution.

Soda Solutions

Strong: Increase the volume of crystals four times by adding water and dissolving (eg top 1 litre of crystals up to 4 litres of liquid).

Standard: Increase the volume eight times by adding water.

Weak: Increase the volume 16 times by adding water.

You can recycle ordinary plastic washing-up liquid bottles by levering off their tops and filling a number of them with strong soda solution all mixed at one time. This is a very convenient way of making sure you have a soda solution ready to hand.

Uses of strong solution

Clearing blocked waste-pipes; cleaning barbecues; freshening drains; cleaning greasy floors and quarry tiles; cleaning smelly bins; removing nicotine stains; cleaning burnt-in grease from pans and casseroles; cleaning brass and pewter; removing green slime from paving stones.

Uses of standard solution

Wiping Venetian blinds clean; washing cane chairs; soaking cleaning cloths before washing; cleaning up after pets; shining basins, baths, loos and bidets; wiping work-tops clean and grease off anything; cleaning squashed insects off car windscreens (rinse afterwards); cleaning cooking hobs, kettles, cutlery and utensils; soaking ink or other stained fabrics before washing; as a cleaning dip for jewellery; cleaning and deodorising chopping boards; cleaning paintwork; soaking out wine stains; soaking slimy sponges; freshening stale-smelling thermos-flasks; detaching chewing gum from furnishings; wiping paraffin (and removing its smell) from oil stoves.

Uses of weak solution

A softening handwash for woollens and delicate hand wash materials; wiping indoor plant leaves; softening brushes and chamois leathers; sparkling glass; cleaning gilt work; wiping lunch boxes and luggage; wiping microwave ovens; soaking net curtains; handwashing quilts; dabbing raincoats and upholstery clean; cleaning vinyl floor and wallcoverings; washing childrens woolly toys.

Other uses of soda crystals

When stewing apples, a pinch in the water stops them going brown; a couple of spoonfuls in a bowl of hard water will soften it; scattered down drains or in the loo they help keep everything fresh and clean; cut flowers last longer with one or two crystals in the water; soiled nappies wash more easily after soaking in water in which crystals have been dissolved.

Information Sources and Further Reading

Books and booklets

Biswas, A K, (Ed), *The Ozone Layer* (for UN Environment Programme, Pergamon, 1979)

Camplin, W C, *Coal Fired Power Stations – The Radiological Impact of Effluent Discharges to Atmosphere* (National Radiological Protection Board, Harwell)

Dotto & Schiff, *The Ozone War* (Doubleday, New York, 1978)

Environmental Effects of Electricity Generation (OECD Publications Office, Paris, 1985)

Handbook of Energy Supply Statistics (The Electricity Council, Annual)

Holmes, A, *Principles of Physical Geology* (Nelson, 1965)

Land Use Policy (Land Use & Climatic Change Edition), Vol 7 No 2, April 1990 (Butterworth Scientific)

McCormick, J, *The User's Guide to the Environment* (Kogan Page, 1985)

Small Scale Agriculture Report 1984 (University of Reading)

Smil, V, *Energy–Food–Environment* (Clarendon Press, Oxford, 1987)

Spedding, C R W (Ed), *Vegetable Productivity* (for Institute of Biology, Macmillan, 1981)

Sugden & West (Ed), *Chlorofluorocarbons in the Environment* (Ellis Horwood, Chichester, 1980)

Tuke, J, *A General View of the Agriculture of the North Riding of Yorkshire drawn up for the Consideration of the Board of Agriculture* (C Nichol, Bookseller, London, 1800)

West, R G, *Pleistocene Geology and Biology* (Longman, 1968)

Papers and articles

Articles in 1990 editions of *The Times* and the *New Scientist*.

Heyworth & Kidson, 'Sea Level Changes in Southwest England and Wales', Department of Geography, University College of Wales.

Hoffman & Zabik 'Effects of Microwave Cooking on Nutrients and Food Systems', *Journal of the American Dietetic Association*, No 8, Vol 85, August 1985

Schneider, S H, 'The Changing Climate', *Scientific American*, September 1989

'The ICI A to Z Guide to Soda Crystals', ICI Homecare, Northwich, Cheshire

Index

Plastics 50, 60
  substitutes for 50
Pollution
  atmospheric, *see*
  Greenhouse effect *and* Ozone
  government inaction on 17
  limits to containment of 17
  measured in cost 18
  water, *see* Water
Population 15, 18
Prepackaging 60, 68

Recycling, *see* Resource saving at
  home
Renewable energy, *see* Energy
Resource saving at home
  animals, with 82, 83
  DIY, by 74, 84
  electronics, by 124
  free time, in 16, 76, 77, 132–4
  gardening, by 77–81
  household audit, by 83, 84
  purchase control, by 84–6, 125,
    131, 132
  recycling, by 16, 59–61, 84,
    124–6, 128, 129
  reduced mobility, by 87, 131
  telecommuting, by 71–4, 125
  timber protection, by 112, 114
  water, of 62, 63, 120, 121, 126
  see also Energy saving at home
    and Waste)

Sales promotion, impact of 85
Salt products 11, 12
Sea levels, rises in 36, 91, 104–6
Sewers and septic tanks 64–7,
  127, 128
Sulphur oxides 26, 27, 30, 40, 94

Third world living standards 14,
  15, 111

Ultra-violet light
  increase in 55, 89–93
  injury from 92, 98, 124, 134

protection against 99, 135
vitamin D and 98

Washing soda
  production of 11, 13
  uses of 64, 66, 121, 138, 139
Waste
  advertising and 67, 84, 85, 131
  attitudes to 67, 68
  commuting and 69–71, 132,
    133
  disease from 57, 58
  domestic:
    gases 57–9
    liquids 62–7
    refuse 57, 59
    solids 59–62, 126
  electricity and 22, 26–30
  fashion and 67, 85, 86
  gardens, in 81, 82
  giveaways and 67, 68
  heat, of 22, 29
  human energy, of 16, 74, 75
  incineration 57–9
  leisure time, in 77, 87
  less obvious aspects of 16, 17
  methane from 39
  nuclear 27–9
  plastics 60
  prepackaging and 60, 68
  recycling, *see* Resource saving
    at home
  sewage and 64–7
  water, in 65, 67
  water, of 62, 63, 126, 127
Water
  bleach in 64–6
  detergents in 64
  domestic use of 62, 63
  oil and solvents in 66
  rainwater, use of 63, 64, 108,
    127
  savings of 62, 63, 120, 121
  solid waste in 66, 127
Weil's disease 58